TRIVIA

I Lov

Don't be "a-Fred" of these mind boggling trivia teasers and have no "Mertz-y" for your friends when you play "I LOVE LUCY TRIVIA MANIA! "Are-nez" you ready for these questions:

– Ricky's piano player was Marco Tork. True or False?
– From whom did the Ricardos purchase their Connecticut home?
– Name the clown who got injured at a rehearsal at the Tropicana?
– What prompted Lucy to attend the radio broadcast of "Females are Fabulous"?
– The Ricardos stayed at the Eden Roc hotel in Miami Beach. True or False?
– Where was Ricky's band booked for a summer-long engagement, forcing them to sublet their apartment?
– Why did Lucy and Ethel have to share a ride to Florida with a total stranger?
– Who arranged the interview with magazine writer Eleanor Harris?
– For an Indian-themed show at the Tropicana, what musical number did Lucy wheedle her way into?
– Adelaide was Mr. Merriweather's late wife. True or False?

For the answers to these and more than 990 other fascinating questions, keep on reading and surrender yourself to . . . TRIVIA MANIA!

I LOVE LUCY

BY XAVIER EINSTEIN

ZEBRA BOOKS
KENSINGTON PUBLISHING CORP.

For Bart Andrews, author of *The "I Love Lucy" Book*

ZEBRA BOOKS

are published by

Kensington Publishing Corp.
475 Park Avenue South
New York, NY 10016

First printing: September 1985

Printed in the United States of America

TRIVIA MANIA:
I Love Lucy

1) Before her TV career began, what radio comedy series did Lucy headline?

2) Name the actor who portrayed Lucy's husband, George, on the radio comedy series she starred in just prior to the debut on TV of I LOVE LUCY.

3) In what play was Vivian Vance appearing when she was discovered for the role of Ethel Mertz by Desi Arnaz?

4) What are the names of the original "Lucy" writers?

5) Name the original sponsor of I LOVE LUCY.

6) I LOVE LUCY was based on a radio show of the same name. True or false?

7) From what state does Lucille Ball hail?

8) During which of the six "Lucy" seasons did Lucy become pregnant?

. . . Answers

1. "My Favorite Husband"

2. Richard Denning

3. *The Voice of the Turtle*

4. Jess Oppenheimer, Madelyn Pugh, and Bob Carroll, Jr.

5. Philip Morris cigarettes

6. False

7. New York

8. The second, 1952–53

9) What department store supplied Lucy's clothes for the first few seasons of the show?

10) What actress portrayed Lucy's nemesis, Caroline Appleby?

11) Name the actor who played Eddie Grant, the lingerie salesman.

12) What was the Munsons' little boy's name?

13) In what city did Fred and Ethel once work at a diner?

14) What did Ethel say she hoped to find in the trunk when she was faced with changing a flat tire?

15) Name the actor who played Ralph Ramsey, Ben Benjamin and Freddie Fillmore.

16) On what day did I LOVE LUCY debut?

17) On what TV network did "Lucy" originally air?

18) At what hotel was Van Johnson appearing?

19) Where was Caroline Appleby headed when she stopped to see Lucy and Ethel in Hollywood?

20) What bridge are the Ricardos and Mertzes crossing when they start singing "California, Here I Come"?

21) How did the Gobloots enter the United States?

. . . Answers

9. Orbach's
10. Doris Singleton
11. Hal March
12. Billy
13. Indianapolis
14. A mechanic
15. Frank Nelson
16. Monday, October 15, 1951
17. CBS
18. The Beverly Palms Hotel
19. Hawaii
20. George Washington Bridge
21. "on the hind legs of the boo-shoo bird"

22) What part did famed TV director Gene Reynolds once play?

23) What song did Ricky sing to hillbilly Lucy on the occasion of Fred and Ethel's wedding anniversary?

24) Who wrote *How to Keep the Honeymoon from Ending?*

25) How many dishes did the girls claim they washed during their marriages in the episode "Pioneer Women"?

26) How many cakes of yeast did Lucy mistakenly put into her homemade bread?

27) Name the highfalutin organization to which Lucy and Ethel yearn to belong.

28) What was the snooper's helper?

29) In a grade school production of *Dance of the Flowers,* what did Lucy play?

30) Name the dance instructor essayed by actress Mary Wickes.

31) Name the spinster neighbor played by Bea Benaderet.

32) Who was Lucy's grocer?

33) What was the value of the fur coat that Lucy mistakenly called her own?

. . . Answers

22. A newlywed who rented the Ricardo apartment after they moved to New England

23. "Guadalajara"

24. Dr. Humphreys

25. 219,500

26. 13

27. Society Matrons League

28. Furnace pipe

29. A petunia

30. Madame Lamond

31. Miss Lewis

32. Mr. Ritter

33. $3,500

34) Aside from roast pig, what was Ricky's Ricardo's favorite meal?

35) With whom did Ricky dance during the production number "Jezebel"?

36) Name Lucy's four poker-playing cronies.

37) Dressed as Carmen Miranda, what song did Lucy lip-sync to?

38) To what did Ethel once liken Fred's mother's face?

39) Where was Ricky going to duel with a Frenchman?

40) What two parts did character actress Verna Felton portray?

41) Who was Vivian Vance's real-life husband?

42) Where did the War Department tell Ricky to report?

43) According to Lucy, why do they call bank tellers "tellers"?

44) Where did Lucy McGillicudy go to high school?

45) Name the employment agency where Lucy and Ethel land candy factory positions.

46) What was Ethel's first job in the candy factory?

. . . Answers

34. *Arroz con pollo* (chicken and rice)

35. Rosemary

36. Ricky, Fred, Hank, and Charlie

37. *"Mama Yo Quiero"*

38. A weasel

39. Behind Radio City Music Hall

40. Mrs. Porter, the maid; and a woman to whom Lucy tried to sell the vacuum cleaner

41. Philip Ober, an actor

42. Fort Dix, New Jersey

43. Because "they go around blabbing everything they know"

44. In Celeron, New York

45. Acme

46. In the boxing department

47) Which job was not offered to Lucy and Ethel?
a. PBX operator
b. bookkeeper
c. dental hygienist
d. maid

48) What was the foreman's precise command to the conveyor belt operator at the candy factory?

49) Name Mrs. Trumbull's nephew.

50) Mr. Littlefield sold the Tropicana to Mr. Chambers. True or false?

51) At first, I LOVE LUCY was a live show. True or false?

52) I LOVE LUCY was telecast on Monday nights. True or false?

53) Who directed more "Lucy" episodes than anyone else?

54) Name the two designers who created Lucy's clothes.

55) With what episode did the Ricardos gain a window behind their piano?

56) What do Mr. Stewart, Mr. O'Brien, and Mr. Foster have in common?

57) The Mertzes' dog was named Butch. True or false?

58) In what apartment did the Mertzes reside?

. . . Answers

47. d. maid

48. "Speed it up!"

49. Joe

50. True

51. False

52. True

53. William Asher

54. Elois Jenssen and Edward Stevenson

55. "The Ricardos Change Apartments"

56. They were all tenants in the Mertz apartment building

57. True

58. 3-A

59) How many episodes of I LOVE LUCY are in syndication?

60) Name Mr. Littlefield's wife.

61) What piece of jewelry did Ricky give Lucy for her anniversary?

62) Before joining The Wednesday Afternoon Fine Arts League, to what women's club did Ethel belong?

63) Name the twins Lucy babysat for.

64) What song did Lucy perform with twin boys for an amateur contest?

65) Desi Arnaz is more than six years younger than Lucille Ball. True or false?

66) Fred suffered from seasickness. True or false?

67) What did Ethel want earnestly for her birthday?

68) What did Ethel come to borrow the day the fan magazine interviewer arrived at the Ricardos'?

69) Who was Theodore?

70) Name the year and make of car that brought the Ricardos and Mertzes to California.

71) Who ran the music school where Little Ricky attended?

. . . Answers

59. 179

60. Phoebe

61. Pearls

62. The Middle East 68th Street Women's Club

63. Timmy and Jimmy Hudson

64. "Ragtime Cowboy Joe"

65. True

66. True

67. Toaster

68. A cup of half 'n' half

69. A dog

70. 1955 Pontiac convertible

71. Mr. Crawford

72) Why did Lucy have to replace ukulele player Earl Robie?

73) What episode introduced Mrs. Trumbull?

74) What excuse did Lucy give for not having any baby formula on the transatlantic flight?

75) What lyrical line follows "I am the good king Lancelot"?

76) Who were the "Communists" living in the Mertz apartment building?

77) Name the salad dressing Lucy and Ethel were hawking.

78) How old was Lucille Ball when I LOVE LUCY premiered?

a. 30
b. 34
c. 36
d. 40

79) How old was Vivian Vance when I LOVE LUCY began?

a. 35
b. 39
c. 45
d. 50

80) On what day was Little Ricky born?

81) What incident that occurred in the fall of 1953 threatened to shut down production on I LOVE LUCY?

. . . Answers

72. The boy contracted the measles the night of the show

73. "No Children Allowed"

74. "He's too fat anyway!"

75. "I like to sing and dance a lot"

76. A husband-and-wife team of actors, the O'Briens

77. Aunt Martha's Old-Fashioned Salad Dressing

78. d. 40

79. b. 39

80. January 19, 1953

81. Lucy was falsely accused of being a Communist

82) Eighteen years before I LOVE LUCY, Lucille Ball arrived in Hollywood as a starlet to make what Goldwyn film?

83) On what film did Lucy and Desi meet?

84) What film, based on a Clinton Twiss book, did the Arnazes make in 1953 during an I LOVE LUCY hiatus?

85) Eve Arden appeared in what I LOVE LUCY episode?

86) From what Marx Brothers movie was the "invisible" mirror routine borrowed?

87) What was Lucy doing while Charles Boyer smothered her with kisses?

88) What happened when Lucy asked Charles Boyer for his autograph?

89) When Lucy played the Mertzes' maid, what name did she use?

90) The night the Littlefields invited the Ricardos for dinner, what was the menu?

91) How did Lucy bribe Caroline Appleby into nominating her for president of the Wednesday Afternoon Fine Arts League?

92) Where did Lucy and Ethel cavort as Martians?

. . . Answers

82. *Roman Scandals*

83. *Too Many Girls*

84. *The Long, Long Trailer*

85. "L. A. at Last," a/k/a "Bill Holden"

86. *Duck Soup*

87. Peeling and eating an orange

88. She squirted ink on his clothing

89. Bessie

90. Pork chops, baked potato, and asparagus tips with Hollandaise sauce

91. By giving her her new cashmere sweater and handbag

92. Atop the Empire State Building

93 What did Lucy name her cheese-baby?

94) What airline did the Ricardos and Mertzes use to come home from Europe?

95) What prevented Ricky and Fred from seeing the Hollywood Stars baseball game the day Lucy and Ethel were in Palm Springs?

96) Lucy's date at Ciro's in Hollywood was Bobby the bellboy. True or false?

97) The Mertzes were experienced in what field of entertainment?

98) What was the name of the twins' frog?

a. Herman
b. Leonard
c. Elmer
d. Froggie

99) What did Mr. Meriweather do for a living?

100) Who was Tillie?

101) Translate the following *Variety* headline: PARKER PREPS PROD FOR PITT PREEM.

102) Name the song that identifies Lucy to her Jamestown family doctor.

103) What was Ethel's maiden name?

104) Name the rotund twins that the Ricardos and Mertzes encounter in Tennessee.

. . . Answers

93. Chester, nee Cheddar

94. Pan American World Airways

95. A rainstorm

96. False, it was Mocambo

97. Vaudeville

98. c. Elmer

99. Broadway producer

100. Mr. Meriweather's cocker spaniel

101. Parker Prepares Production for Pittsburgh Premiere

102. "Skip to My Lou"

103. Potter

104. Teensy and Weensy

105) Name the central characters in "Over the Tea-cups."

106) What Broadway musical did the Ricardos and Mertzes enjoy?

107) Where did Fred live when he moved out on Ethel?

108) What make of automobile did Fred buy for the transcontinental trip?

109) How did Lucy, dressed as Superman, get locked out on the ledge of the apartment?

110) Name the Italian town where Lucy went to "soak up local color."

111) To what did the grape vineyard foreman liken the size of Lucy's feet?

112) The Ricardos visited Venice on their European trip. True or false?

113) Ethel discards Fred's old sweatshirt. What was written across the front of the shirt?

114) How many radio quiz shows did Lucy appear on?

115) What was Freddie Fillmore's profession?

116) Dressed as a hillbilly, Lucy graced the cover of what popular magazine?

117) What year were Lucy and Ricky married?

. . . Answers

105. John and Cynthia

106. *The Most Happy Fella*

107. Y.M.C.A.

108. Cadillac

109. Prospective tenants locked the access window of a vacant apartment

110. Turo

111. Pizza pies

112. True

113. Golden Gloves of 1909

114. Three

115. Quizmaster

116. *Look*

117. 1940

118) How is Ricky's name spelled on his marriage license?

119) What class of train ticket did Ricky buy for the Mertzes' trip back East?

120) Who married the Ricardos a second time?

121) What song was sung at Lucy and Ricky's second wedding ceremony?

122) What was Lucy's middle name?

123) What was Fred's middle name?

124) Name the film that producer Murdoch was making.

125) Name the tour bus Lucy boarded to get a glimpse at the stars' homes.

126) During her first driving lesson, where did Lucy try to make a U-turn?

127) Name the fan magazine writer who interviews the Ricardos for a story about an "average day in the life of Lucy and Ricky."

128) Who was Carlota Romero?

129) Name the actor who played Bill Parker and Bill Sherman.

130) Who was Dr. Harris?

. . . Answers

118. Bicardi

119. Upper berths

120. Bert Willoughby

121. "I Love You Truly"

122. Esmerelda

123. Hobart

124. *Moon Over Baghdad*

125. Grayline Bus Tours

126. In the Holland Tunnel

127. Eleanor Harris

128. A singer from Ricky's past who was appearing in New York and of whom Lucy became jealous until she met the heavyset entertainer

129. Dayton Lummis

130. The doctor who delivered Little Ricky

131) On what occasion did the Ricardos give the Mertzes a new TV set?

132) Who shared the father's waiting at the hospital with Ricky?

133) On what occasion does Little Ricky have to go to the hospital?

134) What is Ricky's answer to the quiz show query: "What is the name of the animal that fastens itself to you and drains you of your blood"?

135) Where does Lucy, as the Maharincess, take up residence?

136) Where did Lucy and Ethel get the walk-in meat freezer?

137) Who was Renita's dance partner?

138) What was Carlos and Maria's last name?

139) From whom do Lucy and Ethel buy 700 pounds of meat?

140) Why does Lucy have a closetful of silverware and other valuables that do not belong to her?

141) Where did Lucy claim she stole the baby elephant?

142) Who calls Lucy, "Red"?

. . . Answers

131. Their 25th wedding anniversary

132. Mr. Stanley, father of six girls

133. To have his tonsils removed

134. "The director of the Internal Revenue"

135. At the Waldorf-Astoria Hotel

136. From Ethel's Uncle Oscar

137. Ramon

138. Ortega

139. Johnson Meat Company

140. She is collecting them for a club bazaar

141. From the Clyde Beatty Circus

142. Mr. Ritter, the amorous grocer

143) What did John Wayne's friends, including Ricky, call him?

144) According to Ethel, what does Ricky have—aside from a band and a reputation—that Lucy does not?

145) What makes Ricky and Fred believe Lucy and Ethel are expecting babies?

146) Who is the nephew of the woman who runs the French hand laundry?

147) After re-styling a fur coat, what remark does Lucy make to Ethel who is modeling the creation?

148) Why does Ricky bring home a mink coat?

149) When Lucy divides the apartment in half, who got the bathroom?

150) In "Men Are Messy," to what does Lucy liken the living room after Ricky arrives home and makes a mess of it?

a. cyclone
b. tornado
c. storm
d. earthquake

151) Where did Lucy win a new set of furniture?

152) Name the two roles that actor Hans Conried played.

153) Who made up the word "dauncey"?

. . . Answers

143. Duke

144. Talent

145. The girls are knitting

146. Jean Valjean Raymond

147. "Congratulations, Ethel. You're the first woman ever to wear a mink T-shirt"

148. It was a prop for a production number at the Tropicana

149. Ricky

150. a. cyclone

151. At the Home Show

152. Secondhand furniture dealer Dan Jenkins, and English tutor Mr. Livermore

153. Lucy's grandmother

154) How many times did the girls claim they went to the Club 21?

155) When Lucy is forced to tell the truth, what age does she claim to be?

156) What was Caroline Appleby's husband's name?

157) What did Caroline Appleby's husband do for a living?

158) According to Lucy, on what occasions does infant Ricky speak Spanish?

159) Who "scratches himself and peels bananas with his feet"?

160) What style of living room furniture did Caroline Appleby buy?

161) Which friend does Lucy accuse of "cackling"?
   a. Caroline Appleby
   b. Ethel Mertz
   c. Marion Strong
   d. Grace Munson

162) What prompted Ricky to put Lucy on a strict time schedule?

163) The meat company arrives with the two sides of beef cut into steaks, chops, etc. True or false?

164) What role did Ricky play in Little Ricky's school pageant?

. . . Answers

154. Four

155. 33

156. Charlie

157. He ran a TV station

158. "Only when he's mad"

159. Caroline Appleby's son Stevie

160. Chinese Modern

161. c. Marion Strong

162. She caused them to be late for a dinner at the Littlefields'

163. True

164. A hollow tree

165) How many children did Lucy claim she had when Mr. Ritter continued to make passes at her?

a. 25
b. 12
c. 7
d. 10

166) Name the TV host played by Frank Nelson.

167) What was the name of the Edward R. Murrow-like TV commentator?

168) Who sponsored "Breakfast with Lucy and Ricky"?

169) Near what Ohio city was the rickety motel where the Ricardos and Mertzes spent a night?

170) Whose pralines didn't the foursome enjoy on their trip to California?

a. Aunt Peggy's
b. Aunt Pauline's
c. Aunt Racine's
d. Aunt Sally's

171) What was the site of Ethel's homecoming performance?

172) What role did actor Robert Jellison play more than once?

173) What was the "relationship" between Ernest Ford and Lucy Ricardo?

. . . Answers

165. a. 25

166. Dickie Davis

167. Ed Warren

168. Phipps Department Store

169. Cincinnati

170. d. Aunt Sally's

171. Little Theatre in Albuquerque

172. Bobby the bellboy

173. Lucy's mother's friend's roomate's cousin's middle boy

174) What astrological sign was Ricky?

a. Gemini
b. Leo
c. Pisces
d. Virgo

175) If Lucy was a "3" and Ethel was a "7," what was Ricky?

176) What brand of cigars did Uncle Alberto smoke?

177) How much did Lucy weigh when she married?

178) Who fought the Battle of the Argonne Woods?

179) What is a zorch?

180) With what substance did Lucy mistakenly glue on her beard?

181) Why does Lucy tell Ethel, "You look like an ad for a trip around the world"?

182) Lucy received $100 for her fiction writing efforts. True or false?

183) What musical instrument did Caroline Appleby play?

184) What was the title of the sequel to Forever Ember?

185) What was the prize money for the Bonus Buck?

a. $100
b. $200
c. $300
d. $500

. . . Answers

174. a. Gemini

175. A "5"

176. Corona Grande

177. 120 pounds

178. The bum who appeared at the Ricardos' back door in "The Quiz Show"

179. The fictional organ Lucy's "doctor" claimed had to be removed as a result of a case of the gob-loots

180. Bulldog Cement

181. She was wearing a costume made up of Eskimo, Oriental and American Indian garb

182. True

183. Drums

184. *Sugar Cane Mutiny*

185. c. $300

186) What paper did Pete and Sam work for?

187) The female duo of "McGillicuddy and Mertz" sang what song to audition for Ricky's Gay Nineties revue?

188) After mulling the baby names Gregory or Joanne, John and Mary, and Sharon and Pierpont, what choices did Lucy finally make?

189) What was the pattern on the wallpaper that Lucy and Ethel use to redecorate the Ricardo bedroom?

190) Name the schoolboy Lucy tries to teach to dance.

a. Arthur
b. Harold
c. Leonard
d. Herb

191) Who are the Buzzells and the Sedgwicks?

192) What was the female "answer" to "Cuban Pete"?

193) Why did Ricky's dance partner Joanne quit?

194) Ricky institutes a "be a pal" system in order to win back Lucy's affections. True or false?

195) Who was Grace Foster supposedly having an affair with?

196) Why did Ethel once visit Minnesota?

. . . Answers

186. *New York Herald Times Tribune*

187. "By the Light of the Silvery Moon"

188. Robert or Madelyn

189. Stripes

190. a. Arthur

191. The Ricardos' friends

192. "Sally Sweet"

193. She was getting married

194. False, Lucy dreamed up the plan

195. The milkman

196. She had her gallstones removed at Mayo Brothers

197) How much did a replacement steering wheel for the Pontiac cost?

198) For what newspaper did Billy Hackett work?
   a. *Chronicle*
   b. *Gazette*
   c. *Tribune*
   d. *Journal*

199) Who sang "Shortnin' Bread"?

200) Where was the gambling casino that Lucy and Ethel visited?

201) For whom was the loving cup that Lucy got stuck on her head intended?

202) According to a newspaper item Lucy reads, what musician is the Shah of Persia crazy about?

203) What was "Raggedy Ricky"?

204) Who was Mr. Estes?

205) Who played Jerry the agent?

206) Aside from her husband and the Mertzes, to whom did Lucy say, "That's a swell way to get off to a lousy start"?

207) What kind of a store did William Abbott operate?

. . . Answers

197. $16

198. a. *Chronicle*

199. Ethel

200. Monte Carlo

201. Jockey Johnny Longden

202. Benny Goodman

203. The dummy Lucy fashioned from a rubber replica of Ricky's head

204. The jewelry salesman Lucy mistook for a jewel thief

205. Jerry Hausner

206. Mr. Livermore, the English tutor

207. An art supply shop

208) Name the whodunit book that prompts Lucy to think Ricky may do away with her.

a. *The Deadly Dagger*
b. *Who Killed the Lady of the House*
c. *Finders Keepers*
d. *The Mockingbird Murder Mystery*

209) Name the fairy tale that Ricky tells Little Ricky in Spanish.

210) Who impersonated Maurice DuBois?

211) How much money did Lucy pledge to Cynthia Harcourt's charity drive?

212) Lucy schemes to keep Ricky from judging a beauty contest in Miami. True or false?

213) What two friends became "as thick as thieves"?

214) What exactly was the theatre ticket mixup when the Ricardos and the Mertzes attended a Frank Loesser musical on Broadway?

215) What was the retail price of the salad dressing?

a. 35¢
b. 40¢
c. 45¢
d. 50¢

216) What edible housewarming gift is delivered to the new Ricardo country home from the Mertzes?

217) In Hollywood, Lucy met Jimmy Durante. True or false?

. . . Answers

208. d. *The Mockingbird Murder Mystery*

209. *Little Red Riding Hood*

210. Charles Boyer

211. $500

212. True

213. Ethel Mertz and Betty Ramsey

214. The tickets were for a matinee, not the evening performance

215. b. 40¢

216. A basket of fruit

217. False

218) Who said, "I'm just dying to see those lousy movies again"?

219) What was the exact address of the Mertz apartment building in New York City?

220) When Lucy is taught the classic burlesque routine, "Slowly I Turn," by a veteran clown, what key word causes all the commotion?

221) Name the song the English tutor wished to introduce at Ricky's club.

222) What was the purported budget of Don Juan

a. $1 million
b. $2 million
c. $3 million
d. $4 million

223) What screen-test line came after, "Hark! Do I hear a foot fall?"

224) Name the female crook who menaced the Ricardos' eastside neighborhood.

225) Who was Eve Whitney?

226) What was the original title of Lucy's Cuban-set play?

227) To whom was the sample invitation to the Tropicana that Lucy found in Ricky's coat pocket addressed?

228) Whom does Lucy hire to teach her how to jitterbug?

. . . Answers

218. Fred, on the occasion of Ricky re-showing his home movies

219. 623 East 68th Street

220. Martha

221. "Tippy Tippy Toe"

222. c. $3 million

223. "Is it you, Don Juan?"

224. Madame X

225. Tom Williams' sexy date

226. *A Tree Grows in Havana*

227. Minnie Finch

228. Arthur "King Cat" Walsh

229) What type of act was Ricky negotiating for the day he was determined not to lose his temper?

a. Dance
b. Ventriloquism
c. Acrobatic
d. Musical

230) Which actress was *not* being considered as Ricky's *Don Juan* leading lady?

a. Marilyn Monroe
b. Judy Holliday
c. Yvonne DeCarlo
d. Arlene Dahl

231) Richard Widmark's dog was Skipper. True or false?

232) Ricky's piano player was Marco. True or false?

233) Name the clown who got injured during a rehearsal at the Tropicana.

234) Who commented, "When Lucy plays the saxophone, it sounds like a moose with a head cold"?

a. Caroline Appleby
b. Ricky Ricardo
c. Ethel Mertz
d. Fred Mertz

235) On what TV game show does Lucy try to win a trip to Hawaii?

236) The Ricardos' half of the lucky dollar wound up at the laundry because Lucy forgot to remove it from the pocket of her robe. True or false?

237) What genre of film did Lucy and the Mertzes produce themselves which was later spliced into Ricky's TV show audition?

. . . Answers

229. b. Ventriloquism

230. b. Judy Holliday

231. False, Cap

232. True

233. Buffo

234. c. Ethel Mertz

235. "Be a Good Neighbor"

236. False, from the pocket of Ricky's pajama top

237. Western

238) What song did the Ricardos and Mertzes perform with Ernie Ford on the "Millikan's Chicken Mash Hour"?

a. "Home on the Range"
b. "Birmingham Jail"
c. "Red River Valley"
d. "Y'all Come"

239) From whom did Lucy buy a kitchen gadget for $7.98?

240) For an Indian-themed show at the Tropicana, what musical number did Lucy finally wheedle her way into?

a. "By the Waters of Minnetonka"
b. "Indian Love Call"
c. "Three Little Indians"
d. None of the above

241) Who arranged the interview with magazine writer Eleanor Harris?

242) What was Ethel's middle name?

a. May
b. Roberta
c. Louise
d. All of the above

243) Little Ricky was almost named Romeo. True or false?

244) Name the actor the Ricardos and Mertzes encountered on the desert island.

. . . Answers

238. d. “Y’all Come”

239. Harry Martin

240. a. “By the Waters of the Minnetonka”

241. Jerry

242. d. all of the above

243. True

244. Claude Akins

245) On what floor of the Mertz apartment building did the Ricardos live the longest?

246) Why did Lucy and Ethel have to share a ride to Florida with a total stranger?

247) Who was the "vice president in charge of Ricky Ricardo"?

a. Walter Reilly
b. Dore Schary
c. Ross Elliott
d. Frank Williams

248) Who suggested the chicken-raising scheme as a means of earning extra money?

249) Adelaide was Mr. Meriweather's late wife. True or false?

250) When Lucy looked down Ricky's "colorful" throat, what did she liken the sight to?

a. A rainbow
b. A jar of jellybeans
c. Carlsbad Caverns
d. None of the above

251) When the Ricardos sued the Mertzes in court—and vice versa—whom did the Ricardos retain as their attorney?

252) Where was Ricky's band booked for a summer-long engagement, prompting the Ricardos to sublet their apartment?

. . . Answers

245. Fourth, from 1940 to 1953

246. Lucy misplaced the train tickets

247. a. Walter Reilly

248. Lucy

249. True

250. c. Carlsbad Caverns

251. Ricky

252. Maine

253) In 1954, how much rent were the Ricardos paying?

a. $125
b. $150
c. $175
d. $200

254) What did Lucy want to steal from Richard Widmark's backyard?

255) The Ricardos stayed at the Eden Roc Hotel in Miami Beach. True or false?

256) What was British film producer Sir Clive's last name?

a. Richardson
b. Fredrickson
c. Wilkinson
d. Robertson

257) What pets did Little Ricky own?

a. Frog
b. Goldfish
c. Turtle
d. All of the above

258) From whom did the Ricardos purchase their Connecticut home?

259) When Lucy was accused of changing her mind constantly, what dinner did she order first at the Jubilee restaurant?

260) What did the Mertzes name their half of the diner?

261) Which of Ricky's friends frequented his diner?

a. Alberto
b. Marco
c. Nick
d. All of the above

. . . Answers

253. a. $125

254. A grapefruit

255. True

256. a. Richardson

257. d. all of the above

258. Joe and Eleanor Spaulding

259. Roast beef

260. A Big Hunk of America

261. d. all the above

262) What did the initials G.T.H.P. stand for?

263) What prompted Lucy to attend the radio broadcast of "Females Are Fabulous"?

264) Ricky had brothers in Cuba. True or false?

265) Name the avant garde Parisian fashion designer.

266) On what floor was the Ricardos' room at the Florence, Italy, hotel?

267) What message did Lucy leave for Ricky at the Monte Carlo hotel when she encountered continued problems because of her missing passport?

268) Who was Adele Sliff?

269) What physical malady did the waiter in "Lucy Changes Her Mind" possess?

a. farsightedness
b. stuttering
c. hard of hearing
d. none of the above

270) How many hamburgers did the drunk ultimately order at the diner?

271) If the Mertzes had the "know-how," what did the Ricardos have?

. . . Answers

262. "Going Through Husbands' Pants"

263. Lucy's careless budgeting resulted in Ricky's taking away her charge accounts and Lucy wanted to win the $1,000 jackpot the show awarded winners

264. True

265. Jacques Marcel

266. Fourth

267. "Help!"

268. A script girl that Rock Hudson knew

269. a. farsightedness

270. 100

271. The "name"

272) What was Fred's excuse for not attending the seance?

a. stomach ache
b. tired
c. headache
d. previous engagement

273) What prompted Lucy's arrest in Paris?

274) Looking at the snail in her plate in Paris, what did Lucy say to it?

275) Along with a horse's feedbag, what were Lucy and Ethel's Paris chapeaus made from?

276) What two languages did the drunk that Lucy encountered at the *Bastille* speak?

a. Spanish
b. English
c. French
d. German

277) Fred played the violin. True or false?

278) Ethel could have done what better "with a pitchfork"?

279) How was Bob Hope injured at the baseball game?

280) Who played the part of Diana Jordan?

281) The Ricardos and Mertzes visited Germany on their European tour. True or false?

. . . Answers

272. c. headache

273. Passing counterfeit francs

274. "I think one of your American cousins ate my geranium!"

275. An ice bucket

276. a and d, Spanish and German

277. True

278. Load the new convertible for the trip to California

279. He was struck in the head by a fly ball

280. Barbara Eden

281. False

282) What did Ethel's father do for a living?

283) What was Kildoonan?

284) Name the shoeshine boy befriended by Lucy in an Italian hotel lobby.

a. Carlo
b. Roberto
c. Giuseppe
d. Francesco

285) Who hired Lucy and Ethel to portray Martians?

286) The only song Lucy could play on the saxophone was "Glow Worm." True or false?

287) What was Ricky's reaction upon seeing his newborn son?

288) Why did Lucy visit Schwab's Drugstore?

289) To what legendary screen idol did Mrs. Trumbull liken Ricky?

290) Whose house did the Hollywood tour bus driver describe as having a dollhouse in the backyard?

291) What did Lucy's maid eat for lunch?

a. salad
b. roast beef
c. jelly
d. all of the above.

. . . Answers

282. He ran a sweet shoppe

283. When the McGillicuddy clan in Scotland lived according to a dream sequence episode

284. c. Giuseppe

285. Al Barton

286. False, she could also play "Sweet Sue"

287. He fainted

288. To get discovered for the movies

289. Rudolph Valentino

290. Shirley Temple

291. d. all of the above

292) What was the name of the Salvation Army-type group that Lucy joined?

293) Who ran the charm school that Lucy and Ethel attended?

294) Why did Ricky actually bring home a mink coat?

295) Who worked at Joseff's Jewelry Store?
   a. Bennett Green
   b. Grace Foster
   c. Ruth Knickerbocker
   d. Hazel Pierce

296) Who replaced Ricky at the Tropicana when he quit because Lucy didn't get a raise?

297) What favorite Fred Mertz possession did Lucy ruin in the process of redecorating the Mertz apartment?

298) While publicity photos are being taken of Ricky with four starlets, where was Lucy?

299) Lucy bought Ricky a new conga drum on the occasion of their 13th wedding anniversary. True or false?

300) What did Lucy promise a waiter in return for free French lessons?

301) Name "Cousin" Ernie's hometown.

. . . Answers

292. Friends of the Friendless

293. Phoebe Emerson

294. He wanted to show Lucy the prop he rented for a production number at the Tropicana

295. b. Grace Foster

296. Xavier Valdez

297. His overstuffed chair

298. Trying to get into every photograph

299. False, set of golf clubs

300. A part in a revue at the Tropicana

301. Bent Fork, Tennessee

302) Name Texas oilman Sam Johnson's wife.

a. Gloria
b. Doris
c. Nancy
d. Carol

303) What were Sam and Dorothy's last names?

304) How much more rent did the Ricardos pay when they moved to the larger apartment?

305) Dr. Peterson was the McGillcuddy family doctor. True or false?

306) Where did Ricky and his orchestra appear in London?

307) What Lucy informed her fellow Hollywood tour bus passengers that Ricky was dining with Richard Widmark, the sarcastic bus driver told the assemblage that he would inform whom of that fact?

a. Betty Grable
b. Judy Garland
c. Ann Sothern
d. Lana Turner

308) Whose horseprints did Ethel try her feet out on at Grauman's Chinese Theatre?

309) At the club election, who won the office of presidency?

310) Why did Lucy miss the boat to Europe?

. . . Answers

302. c. Nancy

303. Carter and Cooke, respectively

304. $20 a month

305. True

306. The Palladium

307. d. Lana Turner

308. Trigger's

309. Both Lucy and Ethel—they tied and shared the office

310. She wanted to kiss Little Ricky again

311) The Mertzes owned their apartment free and clear. True or false?

312) For whom did Lucy buy an enormous piece of cheese in Europe?

a. Caroline Appleby
b. Ethel Mertz
c. Mrs. McGillicuddy
d. Mrs. Trumbull

313) What did Lucy sneak into Little Ricky's hospital room to make him feel more at home?

314) What did Will Potter and Bert Willoughby have in common?

315) What sport did Lucy and Ethel take up in the Ricardo living room?

316) Name the Ricardos' laundry service.

317) John Wayne's masseur was George. True or false?

318) Trying to win a trip to Hawaii, what "role" did Lucy play?

a. Fred's mother
b. Ethel's mother
c. Ricky's mother
d. all of the above

319) Who was president of the United States when I LOVE LUCY premiered?

320) Who was head of the Ricardo clan in Cuba?

. . . Answers

311. True

312. c. Mrs. McGillicuddy

313. His teddy bear

314. Both roles were essayed by the same actor, Irving Bacon

315. Basketball

316. Speedy Laundry

317. True

318. b. Ethel's mother

319. Harry S. Truman

320. Uncle Alberto

321) Who claimed that Lucy was a "wicked city woman"?

322) What award did Lucy win aboard the *Constitution*?

323) Who was Johnny Clark?
  a. a TV producer
  b. Ricky's agent
  c. a press agent
  d. a Broadway producer

324) Who danced the most with Diana at the country club?
  a. Ricky
  b. Fred
  c. Ralph
  d. they tied

325) Name the I LOVE LUCY counterpart to Mary Margaret McBride.

326) Ricky's orchestra once rehearsed at the Ricardo apartment. True or false?

327) What elected office did Lucy originally hold in the Wednesday Afternoon Fine Arts League?

328) How many entry blanks did Lucy enter in the Home Show contest for free furniture?

. . . Answers

321. Ernie Ford

322. Ping-pong

323. b. Ricky's agent

324. b. Fred

325. Mary Margaret McMertz

326. True

327. Treasurer

328. 100

329) How much of a deposit did Ricky put down on the New England home?

a. $500
b. $750
c. $1,000
d. $1,500

330) Complete this Lucy spiel—"I have sirloin, tenderloin, T-bone, rump; pot roast, chuck roast, . . ."

331) Expectant Lucy craved ice cream covered with pickles. True or false?

332) Who was the judge at the women's club play competition?

333) Which star's wife did *not* participate in the Hollywood fashion show?

a. Richard Carlson's
b. Dean Martin's
c. Cornel Wilde's
d. Van Heflin's

334) What size TV did the Ricardos present the Mertzes for their anniversary?

335) Ricky's barber was named Nick. True or false?

336) What did Lucy consider the ultimate Hollywood souvenir?

. . . Answers

329. a. $500

330. "ox tail stump"

331. False, she liked sardines on top

332. Darryl B. Mayer

333. c. Cornel Wilde's

334. One with a 19-inch screen

335. True

336. John Wayne's footprints from Grauman's Chinese Theatre

337) For whom was there a phone call at the Brown Derby, causing Fred to leap out of his seat?

a. Ava Gardner
b. Lana Turner
c. Rita Hayworth
d. Marilyn Monroe

338) Name the motion picture discussed during the Alpine conundrum.

339) How many pounds of modeling clay did Lucy buy?

340) What well known song was the accompaniment for Lucy's movie scene?

341) To whom did Lucy and Ethel sell Ricky and Fred's old clothes?

a. Zeb Allen
b. Jeb Allen
c. Clem Allen
d. Jake Allen

342) What film was John Wayne plugging in the episode in which he starred?

343) How did Lucy disguise herself before meeting William Holden?

344) How much did Lucy pay each of the bald men who attended her party?

345) What was the so-called specialty of the house at the motel dining room in Ohio?

. . . Answers

337. a. Ava Gardner

338. *Seven Brides for Seven Brothers*

339. Fifty

340. "A Pretty Girl is Like a Melody"

341. a. Zeb Allen

342. *Blood Alley*

343. She put her hair up in a kerchief, donned glasses, and fashioned a long putty nose for herself

344. $10

345. Cheese sandwich

346) What size was the costume for the "Sally Sweet" production number?

a. 6
b. 8
c. 10
d. 12

347) As insurance, how many extra cement slabs did John Wayne give to Lucy?

348) What did Ricky supposedly have to wear on his head at night to cure his baldness?

349) Stevie Appleby was older than Little Ricky. True or false?

350) Name the Tropicana maitre d' who handled reservations the night Ricky's replacement debuted.

351) Approximately how much furniture did Lucy mistakenly order for her country home?

a. $1,500
b. $2,000
c. $2,500
d. $3,000

352) Mario came to New York from Venice, Italy, to study opera. True or false?

353) Lucy and Ethel played golf with Sam Snead. True or false?

354) Who was Tom Henderson?

. . . Answers

346. d. 12

347. Three

348. A heat cap

349. False. They were the same age

350. Maurice

351. d. $3,000

352. False, he came to see his brother

353. False, Jimmy Demaret

354. An ex-suitor of Lucy's, now owner of a fur salon

355) Why was Mr. Beecher so nervous?

356) Who told Ricky he was going to become "a Cuban Liberace"?

357) Who got a black eye?
 a. Ricky
 b. Fred
 c. Ethel
 d. all of the above

358) What was the theme of the show that Ricky staged for the Queen of England?

359) Who were "a great big bunch of gyps"?

360) Name the Italian film Lucy was hired to perform in.

361) Who played Lily of the Valley in the operetta?

362) How much did the second-hand furniture dealer give Lucy for all of her furniture?
 a. $75
 b. $100
 c. $250
 d. $500

363) With his "sales resistance" at an all-time low, Fred bought Ethel a Handy Dandy refrigerator. True or false?

364) Lucy's inferiority complex first manifests itself when no one laughs at her joke. True or false?

. . . Answers

355. He was a witness at a murder trial

356. Press agent Charlie Pomerantz

357. d. all of the above

358. Circus

359. Phipp's Department Store, according to Lucy

360. *Bitter Grapes*

361. Ethel

362. a. $75

363. False, a washing machine

364. True

365) How did Lucy attempt to convince Ricky that they needed a larger apartment after Little Ricky was born?

366) What liquid was inside the trick drinking glass Lucy gave Ricky to use in the hopes that he would lose his temper first?

367) Where did Mrs. McGillicuddy meet Hedda Hopper?

a. aboard a plane
b. in the hotel lobby
c. in an elevator
d. by the hotel pool

368) Little Ricky starred in a school pageant titled The Enchanted Forest. True or false?

369) Why did the Mertzes suddenly decide against going to Hollywood?

370) Lucy and Ricky spent time in California even before Ricky's acting stint in Don Juan. True or false?

371) What was the name of the health food fanatic so beautifully played by Elsa Lanchester?

372) What was Lucy's "million-dollar idea"?

373) Why was Ethel once called Madame Mertzola?

374) At what movie studio does Lucy finally get an acting job?

. . . Answers

365. She found unusual places to store things and filled the living room with bulky playground equipment, thereby making the room appear smaller

366. Tomato juice

367. a. aboard a plane

368. True

369. They overheard the Ricardos say that they resented the Mertzes always "tagging along" everywhere they went

370. True

371. Mrs. Grundy

372. The salad dressing

373. When she pretended to be a medium

374. M-G-M

375) In what best-selling book did Lucy read that nursery school would not be a good place to send Little Ricky?

376) Name the Lucy Ricardo friend who met Van Johnson.

a. Miriam Van Vleck
b. Marion Strong
c. Hazel Pierce
d. Caroline Appleby

377) On what floor of the Beverly Palms Hotel did the Ricardos and Mertzes live?

a. 2nd
b. 3rd
c. 4th
d. 5th

378) What was unusual about the way Ernie Ford slept on the Mertzes' rollaway bed?

379) Who was Professor Falconi?

380) What three words did the English tutor implore the Ricardos and Mertzes not to say again?

a. krummy
b. lousy
c. swell
d. okay

381) If Lucy was not a "maharincess," what did she claim to be?

. . . Answers

375. *Doctor Spock's Baby Care Book*

376. d. Caroline Appleby

377. b. 3rd

378. He slept on it without opening it fully

379. A knife-thrower

380. b, c, d. lousy, swell, okay

381. A henna-rinsess

382) What did Mr. Littlefield once find in his water glass when dining with Lucy and Ricky?

383) Lucy found a piece of red lace in Ricky's jacket pocket once, leading her to believe that he was having an affair. True or false?

384) How did Lucy try to get the guard at Buckingham Palace to laugh?

385) What song is sung by the barbershop quartet?

386) Name the locksmith who comes from Yonkers to free Lucy and Ricky of handcuffs.

a. Mr. Johnson
b. Mr. Andrews
c. Mr. Watson
d. Mr. Walters

387) What role did actor Allen Jenkins play twice on I LOVE LUCY?

a. a policeman
b. an agent
c. a detective
d. none of the above

388) Why did Fred once remark, "What a relief. I thought he'd never quit"?

389) Who gave the dedication speech on Yankee Doodle Day?

390) How did the baby chicks escape from the den?

. . . Answers

382. A shirt button

383. False, the lace was black

384. She told him a few jokes

385. "Sweet Adeline"

386. d. Mr. Walters

387. a. a policeman

388. When Little Ricky started playing the drums

389. Ricky

390. Little Ricky left the door to the den ajar

391) What type of hunting trip did Lucy and Ricky once experience?

392) "We are knee-deep in a pool of stagnation" refers to what common marital malady?

393) How did Lucy and Ethel spy on Ricky and Grace Foster?

394) What flavor of soup did Lucy serve the Littlefields?

a. Tomato
b. Split pea
c. Chicken
d. Vegetable

395) Where did the Ricardos and Mertzes vacation during the summer of 1951?

396) What line came after "Are you tired, rundown, listless?"

397) Where did the Ricardos and Mertzes once encounter Charles Boyer?

398) Where did Mrs. Mulford work?

a. at a dress shop
b. a fur salon
c. a hat boutique
d. a shoe store

399) Lucy once called Fred a "tightwad" to his face. True or false?

. . . *Answers*

391. Duck-hunting

392. Marital boredom

393. They outfitted themselves in painter's overalls and hoisted themselves up the side of the Mertz apartment building using a scaffold

394. b. split pea

395. Atlantic City

396. "Do you poop out at parties?"

397. In Paris at a sidewalk cafe

398. c. a hat boutique

399. True

00) According to Fred, who did Lucy look like after he gave herself a home permanent?

01) Who was Lucy's high school dramatics coach?

02) How did Fred spell John Wayne's last name when ie tried to "forge" the Duke's signature on a cement lab?

03) Name the make of motorcycle that the Mertzes ntended to drive back to New York on.

04) In which two episodes did Ricky sing "I Get deas"?

a. "Lucy and Ethel Buy the Same Dress"
b. "Lucy and the Dummy"
c. "The Publicity Agent"
d. "Lucy Wants New Furniture"

05) What was Fred's ex-vaudeville partner's name?

06) What prompted Lucy to write a novel?

07) After buying back their old clothes from a junk lealer, Ricky and Fred used boxes from Saks Fifth Avenue. True or false?

08) What did the Ricardos once intend to give Fred or his birthday?

09) What was the washing machine worth to the repairman?

a. $50
b. $60
c. $75
d. $100

. . . Answers

400. Little Orphan Annie

401. Miss Hanna

402. W-A-I-N

403. Harley-Davidson

404. b. "Lucy and the Dummy" and c. "The Publicity Agent"

405. Ted Kurtz or Barney Kurtz, depending on which episode you heard it

406. She read a newspaper account of a housewife who made a fortune writing a book

407. False, from Brooks' Brothers

408. A new tweed suit

409. a. $50

410) What did Mrs. Hansen sell the dress shop for?

411) Who was the first person to assume that Lucy was pregnant?

412) Who played Friar Quinn in the operetta?

413) When the Ricardos and Mertzes spent the evening harmonizing around the piano, what song was their favorite?

414) After the expenses connected with retrieving the lost but lucky buck were paid out of the winnings, how much money was left over?

415) What prevented Lucy from returning to the *Constitution* before it pulled away from the dock?

416) Who was Aunt Yvette?

417) What was Ricky's first name in the Scottish dream-sequence episode?

418) What species of fish did the foursome "catch" in Florida?

419) Little Ricky's case of stage fright was set off when the music school teacher discussed the issue of nervousness. True or false?

420) Why did Ricky change his mind and decide to send Lucy to Florida?

. . . *Answers*

410. $3,000

411. Ethel

412. Fred

413. "Sweet Sue"

414. One dollar

415. Her skirt got caught in the chain of a messenger's bicycle

416. Ethel's fictional French relative

417. "Scotty"

418. Tuna

419. False, the Ricardos and Mertzes discussed nervousness

420. Because he didn't want Lucy to mess up Orson Welles' appearance at the club

21) Name Grace Foster's husband.
  a. Harry
  b. Phil
  c. Bill
  d. Jerry

22) Who received a higher "charm score"—Lucy or thel?

23) How was Lucy dressed when she threw from her edroom window several jugs of her prized henna nse?

24) From what musical piece did the number "My Iero" come?

25) At first, why can't Ricky appear in Fred's Westrn-themed lodge show?

26) Who told the Ricardos that their apartment was a lump"?

27) What roles did Joi Lansing and Jil Jarmyn play in Florida-based episode?

28) While the grownups busy themselves building a arbecue, what diversion kept Little Ricky occupied?
  a. reading
  b. kite-flying
  c. playing cops-and-robbers with Billy
  d. none of the above

29) Who was the Ramsey's son?

. . . Answers

421. c. Bill

422. Lucy

423. She was swathed in bandages

424. *The Chocolate Soldier*

425. He is supposedly booked for a radio show th same day

426. Ricky's new agent

427. Bathing beauties involved in the filming of documentary

428. b. kite-flying

429. Bruce

430) One of Lucy's Hollywood souvenirs was a tin can run over by Cary Grant's rear tire. True or false?

431) How many dishes did Lucy and Ethel once estimate that they had washed during their many years of marriage?

a. 52,900
b. 119,000
c. 219,000
d. 319,000

432) Who was Little Ricky's costar in the school pageant?

433) Who used to babysit for Lucy when she was a baby?

434) What did Fred's ex-vaudeville partner do for a living?

435) Who leered at Lucy, "You're just my type, Red"?

436) What song did Ricky sing after "Rock-a-bye Baby" the night he found out he was going to be a father?

437) What was the posted population of Bent Fork?

a. 101
b. 54
c. 9
d. 79

438) What expensive gift did Ricky present to Lucy for their 13th wedding anniversary?

. . . Answers

430. True

431. c. 219,000

432. Suzy

433. Helen Erickson

434. He was a cook

435. Mr. Ritter, the neighborhood grocer played by Edward Everett Horton

436. "We're Having a Baby"

437. b. 54

438. Stone Marten furs

439) What was Mr. Livermore's first name?

a. Oliver
b. Luther
c. Marion
d. Percy

440) Was Rosemary Ricky's singer or dancer?

441) Where did Ricky go one night in Hollywood on the arm of four gorgeous showgirls?

442) What grocery item did Mrs. Trumbull ask Lucy to buy for her that prompted Ricky to speculate in the stock market?

443) For how long a period of time did the Mertzes and Ricky bet Lucy she couldn't tell a lie?

444) How much does an art critic offer for Lucy's sculptured bust?

445) When the Ricardos moved to the country, Fred agreed to cancel his tenant's lease. For how long was that original lease?

446) The girls may have wanted to go to a nightclub to celebrate the Mertzes' anniversary, but where did they wind up?

447) Name the song Ricky wrote especially for new mother Lucy.

448) Who replaced George Watson in the barbershop quartet?

. . . Answers

439. d. Percy

440. Dancer

441. To a movie premiere

442. All-Pet

443. 24 hours

444. $500

445. 99 years

446. At the fights

447. "There's a Brand New Baby at Our House"

448. Lucy

449) Who wrote the song "Friendship" that Lucy and Ethel sang as the finale of a Wednesday Afternoon Fine Arts League show?

450) What speech "had more performances than South Pacific"?

451) Lucy and Ethel tried to get rid of the unwanted beef they bought by forcing the delivery men into taking it back. True or false?

452) Why did Ricky grow a moustache?

453) Why did Lucy and club cronies decide to form an all-girl orchestra?

a. they wanted to prove to Ricky that they could play as well as his musicians
b. they hoped to raise money for their club
c. they made a bet with the owner of the Tropicana
d. they decided to become musicians

454) What was the color of the wig that Lucy borrowed from her hairdresser to make Ricky jealous?

455) Who was Mr. Cromwell?

456) After Lucy was put on a strict budget by her business manager, how did she manage to have a bundle of extra cash?

457) Who was Ethel Nurtz?

458) What was Angela Randall's real name?

. . . Answers

449. Cole Porter

450. Ethel's statement, "My friendship with the Ricardos means more to me than all the money on earth"

451. True

452. For a potential TV role

453. b. they hoped to raise money for their club

454. Black

455. The ad agency executive who hired Lucy and Ricky for a morning TV show

456. Her business manager opened a charge account at the local grocery market so Lucy began charging all her neighbors' groceries and pocketing their money

457. The character that resembled Ethel Mertz in Lucy's novel

458. Angela Richardson

459) Who played Ross Elliott, the director of the Vitameatavegamin commercial?

460) How does Mrs. McGillicuddy and Little Ricky get to California?

461) Who was Ricky's so-called "fashion consultant"?
   a. Jerry
   b. Fred
   c. Lucy
   d. Ethel

462) When the Ricardos redecorated the Mertzes' apartment, what name did Lucy give the session?

463) What part of Lucy's anatomy was visible in a photo in the *Life* magazine story about Ricky?

464) With whom did Lucy and Ethel try to pair up Eddie Grant?
   a. Grace Munson
   b. Grace Foster
   c. Sylvia Collins
   d. Diana Jordan

465) What did Ricky give Lucy for her birthday?

466) When Ricky came down with a bad case of laryngitis, how did he manage to communicate with Lucy?

467) What was the name of the "Queen of the Gypsies" in the operetta?

. . . Answers

459. Ross Elliott

460. By plane

461. b. Fred

462. A painting party

463. Her left elbow

464. c. Sylvia Collins

465. A song

466. He used a blackboard

467. Camille

468) How did Lucy audition for Ricky when he needed a girl to do a commercial for his TV show?

469) How much did a Jacques Marcel original cost?

470) Lucy snagged George Reeves for Little Ricky's birthday party because Charlie Appleby was a friend of his agent. True or false?

471) Where did Lucy purchase the wax tulips?

a. Garden Shop
b. Westport Gifts
c. Village Gift Shop
d. Westport Nursery

472) What did Lucy mistakenly call Uncle Alberto in Spanish?

473) Who was Rattlesnake Jones?

474) Where did Lucy hide the cheese she bought in Europe?

475) When Lucy first met John Wayne, why was she so embarrassed?

476) What did Lucy have for lunch at the Brown Derby?

477) Why was Ricky stopped by a sheriff while driving in Tennessee?

478) What was the color of the Cadillac Ricky intended to buy with his oil profits?

. . . Answers

468. She removed the innards of a TV set and got inside, then did an act as Johnny from the Philip Morris commercials

469. $250

470. False, Ricky knew him

471. c. Village Gift Shop

472. A fat pig

473. A friend of Fred's who helped the gang put on the rodeo show

474. In Ricky's musicians' instruments

475. Her hair was set in pin curlers

476. Spaghetti with meat sauce

477. He was exceeding the speed limit

478. Periwinkle blue

479) What commission did Lucy and Ethel agree to pay Caroline Appleby per jar of salad dressing?

480) According to Lucy, "next to sugar," what was "Cuba's biggest export"?

481) Who gave Lucy her baby shower?

482) How much did Lucy pay the milkman to play along with the "gossip" gag?

483) Who was responsible for Lucille Ball's makeup?

484) How did Lucy describe her watercress sandwich?

485) How much did Fred spend to buy the motorcycle he intended to drive back to New York from Hollywood?

486) Where did Fred send Ricky's band instead of to Lucerne, Switzerland?

a. Locarno
b. Zurich
c. Lausanne
d. Langnau

487) Fred paid $300 for the old clunker car he bought to travel to Hollywood in. True or false?

488) After paying off her debts, how much of the first month's allowance that Lucy received from her business manager did she have left?

489) What dinner did Lucy cook for Dorothy and Sam?

. . . Answers

479. Three cents

480. Ham

481. The members of the Wednesday Afternoon Fine Arts League

482. Five dollars

483. Hal King of Max Factor

484. "buttered grass"

485. $50

486. a. Locarno

487. True

488. $5

489. Chicken

490) The real estate lady who attempted to sublet the Ricardo apartment was Mrs. Hammond. True or False?

491) Why did Ricky travel free to Europe?

492) Where did Ricky say he was having a Hollywood anniversary party for Lucy?

b. Mocambo
b. Moulin Rouge
c. Ciro's
d. Earl Carroll's

493) What was Fred's "annoying little habit"?

494) What scheme did Ricky's press agent dream up to land Ricky in Hedda Hopper's column?

495) How many laying hens did the Ricardos exchange for their chicks?

496) What was Lucy's miniscule role in the audition song "Auf Wiedersehn"?

497) How many cakes of yeast did Lucy's homemade bread recipe call for?

a. One
b. Two
c. Three
d. Four

498) What did Ricky try to cook that prompted Lucy to exclaim, "He said the charcoal would be good for the baby's teeth"?

. . . Answers

490. True

491. His orchestra played aboard the ship for free

492. a. Mocambo

493. Jingling loose change in his pocket

494. Lucy was to fall into the hotel swimming pool, feign drowning, and then have Ricky save her

495. Six dozen

496. She sang the "auf" in each stanza, nothing else

497. c. Three

498. Waffles

499) Lucy's maid was in complete charge of Little Ricky. True or false?

500) In the show, "Equal Rights," what did Ricky call the waiter?

501) Why did Lucy and Caroline get into an argument over Little Ricky's birthday party?

502) Who were "Fingers" and "The Brains"?

503) Why did Lucy and Ricky suddenly have to dance the tango while she had eggs stuffed in her jacket?

504) Where did Lucy hide the roast chicken in Paris?

505) In what episode did the Ricardos introduce "The Nurtz to the Mertz Mambo"?

506) How much money did Lucy and Ethel earn playing Martians?

507) How were Lucy and Ethel going to "share" John Wayne's cement footprints?

508) What was the name of the escaped hatchet murderess?

a. Evelyn Bigsbee
b. Evelyn Holmby
c. Evelyn Collins
d. Evelyn Farnsworth

509) What was Lucy's relationship to Cynthia Harcourt?

. . . Answers

499. False, Lucy had to care for the baby herself

500. Xavier

501. Caroline's son's birthday party was scheduled for the same day, and both boys had the same guest list

502. Fred and Ricky, respectively, in "Lucy Wants to Move to the Country"

503. A last-minute rehearsal for a PTA show

504. A camera bag

505. "Little Ricky Learns to Play the Drums"

506. $500 each

507. Each would have the slab on alternating weeks

508. b. Evelyn Holmby

509. A school chum

510) Why did Fred once tell Lucy that she "could always enter her head in a flower show"?

511) What did Lucy cook for dinner the night she was trying to hide the new set of living room furniture from Ricky?

512) Name the actor who played the animal-hating neighbor.

513) What did lonely Lucy jokingly name the *S.S. Constitution*?

514) What prevented Lucy from easily gaining entry to the French Riviera?

515) Aside from a basket of fruit, what did the Mertzes give to the Ricardos as a country housewarming gift?

516) What magazine asked Lucy to write an article?
  a. *Modern Screen*
  b. *McCall's*
  c. *Saturday Evening Post*
  d. *Photoplay*

517) Why did Lucy slap her candymaking cohort in the face?

518) Lucy won 875,000 francs in Monte Carlo. True or false?

. . . Answers

510. Lucy gave herself a home permanent and came out looking like as she put it, a "chrysanthemum"

511. Steak

512. John Emory

513. *S.S. Noah's Ark*

514. She misplaced her passport

515. A candlestick

516. d. *Photoplay*

517. Because a fly was nearby

518. True

519) What did Lucy want Little Ricky to grow up to be?

a. actor
b. doctor
c. musician
d. lawyer

520) Who played Lucy's "farewell dirge"?

521) Complete the Lucy line that began, "Food always tastes different when they fix it."

522) From what fabric was the outfit that Lucy wore at the Hollywood fashion show made?

523) What film was William Holden promoting in "L.A. at Last"?

524) How often did the two-headed dragon eat?

a. Every 10 years
b. Every year
c. Every 30 years
d. Every month

525) Lucy "learned" to play the saxophone because she once was in love with a football player. True or false?

526) Where did the washing machine tug-o-war between the Ricardos and Mertzes take place?

527) To whom did Lucy say, "Wouldn't you like to see me die?"

. . . Answers

519. b. doctor

520. Ricky's band

521. "I don't know what they do to it"

522. Wool tweed

523. *The Country Girl*

524. c. every 30 years

525. True

526. On the back porch of the third floor

527. The director of her Hollywood movie

28) What royalty fee was saved when Lucy decided to rite her own operetta?

29) What unusual method did Lucy employ to get a untan in Palm Springs?

30) Where was Ricky when Lucy was appearing in he Heart Fund show?

31) What writing credits remained consistent hroughout the six-year run of LUCY?

32) The morning Lucy went out to find work, Ricky ooked her breakfast. True or false?

33) What was Fred's vaudeville partner's grandson's irst name?

34) Who could "work miracles"?

35) Under what circumstances were Lucy and Ethel rrested for robbery?

36) Who moved into the Mertz apartment building irst—Mrs. Benson or Mrs. Trumbull?

37) In what episode did Lucy portray Princess Loo-Cee?

38) Who were the Yankees playing when Bob Hope ttended the same baseball game as Lucy and the Mertzes?

. . . Answers

528. $100

529. She wore a big sun hat, a long robe, and huge sunglasses

530. He was deep sea fishing

531. Bob Carroll, Jr., and Madelyn Pugh

532. False, he bought it at the drugstore

533. Barney

534. Phoebe Emerson's Charm School

535. They were caught red-handed "stealing" from a diner's cash register

536. Mrs. Benson

537. "Lucy Meets Orson Welles"

538. Cleveland Indians

539) What two "Lucy" roles did actress Kathryn Card play?

540) Why did Lucy refer to herself as "Lucy Friml"?

541) How many different sofas did the Ricardos own during the 5 ½ seasons they resided in New York City?

a. 2
b. 3
c. 4
d. 5

542) Where were the Mertzes going to exchange their U.S. dollars for francs?

543) What did Ethel Mertz and Betty Ramsey have in common?

544) Who sported a hairdo that was likened to "a wet Pekinese"?

545) What activity were the Mertzes involved with while Little Ricky's birthday party was in progress?

546) Ethel played a fairy princess in Little Ricky's school play. True or false?

547) To whom did Ricky once sing "Cuban Cabby"?

a. Mrs. Knickerbocker
b. Lucy
c. Ethel
d. Maggie, the Tropicana maid

. . . Answers

539. Minnie Finch and Mrs. McGillicuddy

540. She was going to write an operetta

541. c. 4

542. At the American Express office

543. They were both from Albuquerque, New Mexico

544. Ethel

545. They were trying to rent a vacant apartment

546. True

547. a. Mrs. Knickerbocker

548) What did the young Taylors want to do with Lucy's coffee table?

549) Who was known to repeat the phrase, "You didn't ask me"?

550) There were no animals allowed aboard the *Constitution.* True or false?

551) Name the actress pictured in the Italian film magazine Lucy had in her hotel room.

a. Gina Lollobrigida
b. Sophia Loren
c. Anna Magnani
d. Monica Vitti

552) What was Lucy dipping crackers in when she was reading a murder mystery?

553) How did Ethel render Ben Benjamin unconscious?

554) What did Lucy do with Ricky's breakfast the second day she was on a time schedule?

555) Why did Lucy once masquerade as a bass fiddle?

556) In what LUCY episode did both Vivian Vance and William Frawley not appear?

a. "Lucy Plays Cupid"
b. "The Amateur Hour"
c. "The Audition"
d. "The Seance"

. . . Answers

548. Paint it black

549. Mrs. McGillicuddy

550. False, two dogs appeared in one scene

551. c. Anna Magnani

552. Cold cream

553. She hit him over the head with a vase

554. She cooked it the night before, put it in the freezer, and then served it to him frozen

555. She was trying to gain admittance to the club, against Ricky's strict orders

556. a. "Lucy Plays Cupid"

557) A palm tree broke Lucy's sudden fall from the balcony of her Hollywood hotel suite. True or false?

558) Where did Lucy catch the helicopter that took her out to sea to catch the ship bound for Europe?

559) Where did the handcuffs come from?

560) What was wrong with the coffee table that Lucy sold to the secondhand furniture dealer?

561) Name the book that suggested the "be a pal" system.

562) Whom did Ricky once fire—Marilyn or Joanne?

563) Who said Mabel Normand and Conway Tearle would become big TV stars?

a. Lucy
b. Ricky
c. Jerry
d. Charlie

564) Whose baby bottle did Lucy drink from on the plane trip home from Europe?

565) On what game show did Lucy sing "My Bonnie Lies Over the Ocean"?

566) What animal did Lucy impersonate when she played a set of horns at the Tropicana?

567) What instrument did the Professor play first?

. . . Answers

557. True

558. Idlewild Airport

559. Fred had them

560. It had a loose leg that ultimately fell off

561. *How to Keep Your Honeymoon from Ending*

562. Marilyn

563. d. Charlie

564. Madelyn Bigsby, an infant

565. "Females Are Fabulous"

566. A seal

567. A cello

568) How much did the diner cost?
   a. $1,000
   b. $2,000
   c. $3,000
   d. $4,000

569) Who was Scarlett Culpepper?

570) Why did Lucy visit a store that specialized in hair-restoration preparations and devices?

571) What kind of review was Ricky staging in "Pioneer Women"?

572) How much profit did Lucy and Ethel hope to make on their enormous meat purchase?

573) What movie star touched an orange that Lucy picked up at the Farmers' Market?

574) What episode featured a woman who sang like a chicken?

575) In order for Lucy to acquire a new hat, what did she have to get Ricky to do?

576) When Ricky agreed not to use public transportation in "Pioneer Women," how did he get home from the club?

577) Maria was Giuseppe's relative. True or false?

. . . Answers

568. b. $2,000

569. One of the people Lucy impersonates in "Ricky Asks for a Raise"

570. Ricky thought he was going bald

571. Gay Nineties

572. Ten cents

573. Robert Taylor

574. "Lucy Tells the Truth"

575. Lose his temper

576. By horse

577. False, Teresa

578) What word was Harpo Marx trying to get Ricky and Fred to understand?

a. "charity"
b. "benefit"
c. "nightclub"
d. "motion picture"

579) To what was Ricky referring when he said to Lucy, "I'm not sitting with you as long as you have *that*"?

580) Fred and Ethel met the Queen while in London. True or false?

•

581) Which tire went flat on Mrs. Grundy's convertible?

a. right front
b. left front
c. right rear
d. left rear

582) Whom did Lucy try to flatter by saying their head was like a Greek coin?

583) What started the fight in the grape vat?

584) When Ricky forgot the date of his wedding anniversary, he phoned the appropriate hall of records for the information. True or false?

585) Lucy once dated a man named Kenneth Hamilton. True or false?

. . . Answers

578. b. benefit

579. The cheese wrapped as a baby

580. False

581. b. left front

582. Ethel

583. Lucy shoved the Italian woman, who then fell into the grapes

584. False, he wired them

585. False, Kenneth Hamilton was a young boy with whom she played table tennis aboard the ship bound for Europe

86) Under what circumstances did Lucy say that she ad "picked a peck of pockets"?

87) In the operetta, Friar Quinn ran a tavern. What vas its name?

88) Why did Lucy clamp handcuffs on herself and Ricky?

89) The deed to the Mertz apartment building was in Ethel's name. True or false?

90) Why did frozen Lucy hurriedly ask to have the lectric blanket turned off?

91) Who impersonated the voice of Adelaide Meriveather?

92) Lucy played Isabella Klump in the Vitameatavegamin commercial. True or false?

93) From what Shakespearean play did Lucy act out a cene with Orson Welles?

94) In whose apartment did Lucy "set knees in"?

95) What significance did the term "Hail, Tiger" ave?

96) Whom did Lucy consider a "hunk"?
   a. William Holden
   b. Bennett Green
   c. Mr. Littlefield
   d. Tom Henderson

. . . Answers

586. A psychiatrist Ricky hired to find out why Luc was truly a kleptomaniac

587. The Inn on the River Out

588. To keep him from going to work so they coul spend a rare evening together

589. True

590. She smelled the smoke of her meat barbecueing

591. Fred Mertz

592. False, she played that character on the sala dressing pitch

593. *Romeo and Juliet*

594. The O'Briens'

595. It was featured in "The Publicity Agent" wher Lucy was the Maharincess of Franistan an Ricky was impersonating the sinister Tiger

596. d. Tom Henderson

597) What were the first two words of the Vitameatavegamin pitch?

598) Most of the guests at Ricky's baby shower brought bottles of beer as gifts. True or false?

599) Where was Ricky Ricardo born?

600) Which of the four principal characters did not have a birthday-theme show?

601) Why was it necessary for Lucy to replace Buffo, the clown?

602) What was Lucy's response to the question, "Is this choice meat?"

603) Why did Lucy get inside the steamer trunk?

604) Who was Eve Whitney's date?
   a. Bill Hall
   b. Tom Henderson
   c. Eddie Grant
   d. Tom Williams

605) What role did character actress Lurene Tuttle once play?

606) Why didn't the vacuum cleaner work when Lucy tried to sell it to the feisty old woman?

. . . Answers

597. "Hello, friends . . ."

598. True

599. Cuba

600. Ricky (Lucy had "Lucy's Last Birthday," Ethel had "Ethel's Birthday," and Fred's birthday was featured in "Too Many Crooks")

601. He fell off his trick bike and injured himself

602. "Ethel, give the little lady her choice"

603. To see if she could fit and stow away to Europe

604. d. Tom Williams

605. President of the Wednesday Afternoon Fine Arts League

606. The woman hadn't paid her electric bill and the utility company shut off her power

07) What prized possession of Fred's did Lucy once steal"?

a. cuckoo clock
b. autographed baseball
c. sweatshirt
d. old handcuffs

08) How did Lucy fake her city pallor?

09) Besides Ricky, who was the only other person uaranteed to go to Europe?

10) The Tropicana had 75 tables. True or false?

11) Which tenant made the biggest fuss about the "no hildren allowed" clause in the apartment lease?

12) What musical instrument did Lucy play in the riends of the Friendless band?

13) Who was the "queen of Delancey Street"?

14) What two problems did Lucy encounter when she vas standing out on the ledge in the "Superman" epiode?

15) Lucy met Ricky on a blind date. True or false?

16) What did Lucy do to the clocks in the Ricardo ome that caused her and Ricky to arrive late at the ittlefields' for dinner?

. . . Answers

607. a. cuckoo clock

608. She dusted talcum powder on her face, arm and hands

609. Fred

610. True

611. Mrs. Trumbull

612. Bass drum

613. Sally Sweet

614. Pigeons and rain

615. True

616. Set them all back one hour

617) What roles did Joseph Kearns, who played Mr. Wilson on DENNIS THE MENACE, essay on LUCY?

618) What item of food did Lucy cup up into tiny pieces before eating it so she could waste time?

a. steak
b. french fried potato
c. carrot stick
d. lima bean

619) Describe the toy that Ricky gave his young son to allay his fears of performing in front of strangers.

620) How did Little Ricky destroy one of John Wayne's cement footprints?

621) According to Lucy, what was Hollywood's "watering hole"?

622) What were the Mertzes doing while Lucy was playing a showgirl in an M-G-M movie?

623) What happened to Ethel in the bathroom of the rickety motel in Ohio?

624) Describe the pecularity of Fred's living room reading lamp.

625) Little Ricky met his father's relatives during a visit to Miami. True or false?

626) What once prompted Fred to say, "Why, Ethel, you're molting"?

. . . Answers

617. The doctor in "The Kleptomaniac" and the theatre manager in "Lucy's Night in Town"

618. d. lima bean

619. A windup bear playing a drum

620. He got on top of it and started playing in it while the cement was still wet

621. Brown Derby

622. Appearing in a different film for an old friend, Jimmy O'Connor

623. A train went by and the toothpaste, intended for a brush, wound up on her face

624. When touched, the shade slowly crept down the base of the lamp

625. False, a visit to Havana, Cuba

626. She and Lucy had just gotten off a poultry truck headed for Florida

627) Of the following storylines, which two were connected?

a. Lucy buys new furniture
b. Lucy goes out for her anniversary
c. Lucy tells the truth
d. Lucy gives herself a home permanent

628) To what was Fred referring when he said to Lucy, "Tell your two Andrews Sisters not to wait up for LaVerne"?

629) Who were Madge and Gordon?

630) According to the song, what was "Scottish" Ricky "in love with"?

631) Who mowed down Lucy's "prized" tulips?

632) What did Fred and Ricky enjoy watching on TV the most?

633) What was the alcoholic content of Vitameatavegamin?

a. 80%
b. 23%
c. 20%
d. 90%

634) Ethel had an aunt named Emmy. True or false?

635) Where did Lucy lose her mother-in-law?

636) How did Lucy and the Mertzes manage the many costume changes in "Ricky Asks for a Raise"?

. . . Answers

627. a and d, Lucy buys new furniture and Lucy gives herself a home permanent

628. Playing a game of poker, naive Lucy had a pair of queens and Fred had another

629. The lead characters from the mystery Lucy and Ricky were reading when Lucy got her black eye

630. "A dragon's dinner"

631. Ricky

632. Boxing

633. b. 23%

634. True

635. On the subway

636. A friend of the Mertzes', Hal King, loaned them a wardrobe trunk

637) Why was Ricky home when Lucy decided to build a barbecue?

638) Dore Schary played himself in an episode of I LOVE LUCY. True or false?

639) Who played Lucy's grocer Mr. Ritter?

640) What did Lucy blame a backache on?

641) A few of Ricky's orchestra members once masqueraded as women. True or false?

642) According to their original game plan, who was entrusted with the job of hailing a taxicab for Lucy's trip to the hospital?

a. Ricky
b. Fred
c. Ethel
d. all of the above

643) How much money did Lucy pay the English tutor?

644) What did Lucy say when she arrived home exhausted after unsuccessfully trying to get rid of the vacuum cleaner?

645) Where was the walk-in meat freezer located?

646) What Lana Turner souvenir did the group manage to secure on their Hollywood trip?

. . . Answers

637. He was on a week's vacation

638. False, Phil Ober played the part of Dore Schary

639. Edward Everett Horton

640. Sleeping on a Phipp's mattress

641. True

642. d. all of the above

643. Nothing

644. "One more hour and they'd have reported the death of another salesman"

645. In the basement of the Mertz apartment building

646. A napkin with her lip-print

647) Name the people who specifically did not remember Lucy's birthday.

a. Mrs. Trumbull
b. Ricky
c. Ethel
d. none of the above

648) How did William Holden unnerve Lucy at the Brown Derby?

649) What happened to Lucy as a result of the diet?

650) Name the symptoms Lucy displayed that manifested her frustration at not being allowed to get into show business.

651) In Hollywood, what "petty little habit" did Lucy display that annoyed her husband and friends?

652) What means of transportation carried the Ricardos and Mertzes to Rome?

a. airplane
b. bus
c. train
d. boat

653) Why did Lucy and Ricky once assume Ricky needed eyeglasses?

654) The Ricardos ran into a counterfeiter in Germany. True or false?

655) What was Lucy eating when "Face to Face" went on the air?

. . . Answers

647. d. none of the above

648. He gave Lucy a taste of her own medicine by staring at her

649. She collapsed after the Tropicana show

650. She reverted to childhood, impersonated a famous person, and had an acute case of amnesia

651. She stirred her coffee incessantly

652. c. train

653. He was getting terrible headaches

654. False, in France

655. A piece of chocolate

656) What did the farmer give the Ricardos and Mertzes for breakfast when they stayed overnight somewhere in the Italian countryside?

657) What main dish did Ricky and the Mertzes eat for dinner when Lucy was on her strict diet?

658) What did Lucy and Ethel finally name their dress shop?

659) Lucy got the loving cup stuck on her head because she claimed it would make a nice hat. True or false?

660) How much was a one-way train ticket from New York City to the Ricardos' home in the country.

661) When Ricky was waving goodbye from the deck of the *Constitution*, whom was he acknowledging besides Mrs. Trumbull, Little Ricky, and Mrs. McGillicuddy?

662) Where did Mrs. Grundy finally dump Lucy and Ethel?

663) In a dream sequence depicting Little Ricky getting older and older, with whom was Ricky appearing on a theatre bill?

664) When Ethel said, "We got fired off our first job," to what was she referring?

665) Outside of what European city was Turo?

. . . Answers

656. Cheese, bread, and—from the farmer's cow—milk

657. Steak

658. Lucy and Ethel's Dress Shop and Ethel and Lucy's Dress Shop

659. True

660. $4.08

661. Lucy

662. At a roadside diner somewhere north of Miami

663. Carlota Romero

664. Her and Lucy's jobs at the candy factory

665. Rome

666) Whom did Lucy accuse of "peeling bananas with his feet"?

667) Why couldn't Lucy sit down at the country club dance?

668) Where was the Vitameatavegamin commercial shot?

a. Television Center
b. Television City
c. Broadcast Center
d. CBS

669) What did the foursome first order at the cafe in the rundown motel in Ohio?

670) Whom did Lucy once say she almost married?

a. Cary Grant
b. Clark Gable
c. Tyrone Power
d. Jimmy Stewart

671) How many TV set raffle tickets were sold?

672) What did Mrs. McGillicuddy promise a New York City bus driver?

673) What article did Lucy once cut out of the newspaper so Ricky wouldn't see it?

674) What character did Rolfe Sedan portray?

675) Approximately how much money did Lucy spend on new furniture for the country house?

. . . Answers

666. Stevie Appleby

667. Her dress was too tight

668. a. Television Center

669. Steak sandwiches

670. a. Cary Grant

671. 3,000

672. That she would never ride a New York City bus again

673. That Ricky had formed an all-girl orchestra

674. The chef at the Parisian sidewalk cafe

675. $3,000

676) Lucy had a sister. True or false?

677) Why did Fred call Ethel "Whirlaway"?

678) Who was hired first—Vivian Vance or William Frawley?

679) Vivian Vance played a cameo role in *The Long, Long Trailer.* True or false?

680) Name the actress who did not appear on the series.

a. Sheila MacRae
b. Barbara Eden
c. Eve Arden
d. Ann Francis

681) Who conducted the Desi Arnaz Orchestra off camera?

682) Desi Arnaz, Jr., was born to Lucille Ball on the same night that Lucy gave birth to Little Ricky. True or false?

683) In what year did the half-hour episodes cease to be produced?

684) Name the production company responsible for the show.

685) Why did Ricky agree to go Alp-climbing?

. . . Answers

676. True

677. She was the back end of a costume horse

678. William Frawley

679. False

680. d. Anne Francis

681. Wilbur Hatch

682. True

683. 1957

684. Desilu

685. To get his mind off the fact that his band was stranded in a different Swiss city

686) Which sitcom ran longer than I LOVE LUCY?
   a. OUR MISS BROOKS
   b. PRIVATE SECRETARY
   c. THE ADVENTURES OF OZZIE AND HARRIET
   d. LEAVE IT TO BEAVER

687) Sam and Dorothy got married. True or false?

688) What show did I LOVE LUCY replace on CBS in 1951?

689) In what episode did a chandelier wind up on Fred's head?

690) Aaron Spelling appeared in an episode of I LOVE LUCY. True or false?

691) Desi Arnaz was under 35 years of age when I LOVE LUCY premiered. True or false?

692) In what episode did Lucy refer to her fingers as "Chinese back-scratchers"?

693) In what year were the Ricardos married?
   a. 1938
   b. 1940
   c. 1945
   d. 1951

694) Mr. and Mrs. Harry Martin were once tenants in the Mertz building. True or false?

. . . Answers

686. c. "The Adventures of Ozzie and Harriet"

687. True

688. Horace Heidt

689. "Break the Lease"

690. True

691. True, he was 34

692. "Lucy Visits Grauman's"

693. b. 1940

694. False, Harry Martin was the Handy Dandy salesman

695) Lucy's wedding ring was once found in some ground beef. True or false?

696) Who once reacted to Ricky's assertion that Lucy was acting "crazy" by saying, "Crazy for Lucy, or crazy for normal people?"

697) Name the Ricardos' attorney.

698) Who composed the musical theme song?

699) William Frawley won an Emmy for his role as Fred Mertz. True or false?

700) What episode featured a helicopter scene?

701) What role did Janet Waldo play on I LOVE LUCY?

702) What did Fred advertise on his shirt during the "Face to Face" broadcast?

703) Who liked the bedroom cool at night—Lucy or Ricky?

704) The Ricky Ricardo Orchestra featured a female harpist. True or false?

705) What ex-husband of Tallulah Bankhead made two appearances on I LOVE LUCY?

706) In what episode did Ricky order pizza?

707) How many times were Ricky and Fred jailed?

. . . Answers

695. True

696. Fred

697. They had none

698. Eliot Daniel

699. False, he was nominated four times, but never won

700. "Bon Voyage"

701. Peggy Dawson, the teenage girl who had a crush on Ricky

702. Apartments for rent

703. Lucy

704. True

705. John Emory

706. "Equal Rights"

707. Three—in "New Neighbors," "Equal Rights" and "Tennessee Bound"

708) Who was the actress who appeared once on I LOVE LUCY and later played a supporting role on THE LIFE OF RILEY?

709) What song was Ethel singing in "Redecorating the Mertzes' Apartment"?

a. "Sweet Sue"
b. "She'll Be Comin' 'Round the Mountain"
c. "Lily of the Valley"
d. "Happy Birthday"

710) How did Ethel acquire the bonus buck?

711) What song did Harpo Marx play on his harp?

712) While playing bridge at Caroline Appleby's, who arrived wearing a new hat?

713) While appearing on television, why did Lucy plead, "Cancel, cancel"?

714) What significance did the two swords have in "Lucy Goes to Scotland"?

715) What did Lucy use a catcher's mitt for in "Lucy's Schedule"?

716) Lucy and Ethel once claimed they had dates with Little Boy Blue and Little Jack Horner. True or false?

717) How did Lucy try to get Ethel's fingerprints the day she suspected her of being Madame X?

718) What was Lucy's best bird-call?

. . . Answers

708. Gloria Blondell

709. c. "Lily of the Valley"

710. The grocery delivery boy gave it to her as change after getting the bill from Lucy Ricardo in payment for her groceries

711. "Take Me Out to the Ball Game"

712. Marion Strong

713. To get viewers to stop buying the salad dressing

714. To test her legitimacy as a McGillicuddy, Lucy had to dance a special dance around the swords

715. To catch hot biscuits Ethel was throwing her

716. False, Little Boy Blue and Peter Cottontail

717. On a silver cigarette case, on a drinking glass, and on the steam of a candy dish

718. Cuckoo

19) Who originated the saying, "Never do business ith friends or relatives"?

20) Lucy tried to make a right-hand turn in the Holnd Tunnel. True or false?

21) Why was the chef at the sidewalk cafe in Paris so pset with Lucy?

22) Who gave Lucy and Ricky their silver?

23) In what episode did Lucy and Ethel impersonate Lucy the Lip" and "Baby Face Ethel"?

24) Lucy once said she wasn't the "champagne and aviar" type. What type did she confess to be?

25) What kept the identical tunas fresh?

26) What song did Ricky and Little Ricky duet in Iavana?

27) Where did Lucy encounter Orson Welles?

28) What sport did Lucy and Ethel take up in the Riardos' living room when they feared becoming "golf idows"?

29) When did Ricky spank Lucy to the beat of "Baalu"?

30) According to Fred in the episode "The Diner," hat two songs did Ricky know?

. . . Answers

719. Ricky's father

720. False, a U-turn

721. She wanted to put catsup on her snails

722. Ricky's mother

723. "The Kleptomaniac"

724. The "beer and pretzel" type

725. Ice cubes

726. "Babalu"

727. At Macy's

728. Basketball

729. In "Ricky's *Life* Story," when Lucy upstaged Ricky

730. "Babalu" and "You Got the Know-How, I Got the Name Blues"

731) What did "kleptomaniac" Lucy pick from the psychiatrist's pocket?

732) How old was Little Ricky when the Ricardos celebrated his birthday *in absentia* in Italy?

a. 2 years old
b. 3 years old
c. 4 years old
d. 5 years old

733) Aside from crackers, what did Lucy eat in bed in an attempt to get Ricky to lose his temper?

734) Who was Van Johnson's regular dance partner?

735) In "The Black Wig," who were Doug and Roberta?

736) How did Mrs. Hansen trick Lucy and Ethel into paying her original asking price for the dress shop?

737) Lucy shared the driving chores with Mrs. Grundy. True or false?

738) What was Mario's last name?

a. Martinelli
b. LaGreca
c. Troiano
d. Orsatti

739) Who asked Lucy, "Do you ouija?"

. . . Answers

731. A watch

732. b. 3 years old

733. Nuts

734. Hazel

735. Lucy's hairdressers

736. She concocted a series of classic sob stories

737. False

738. d. Orsatti

739. Mr. Merriweather

40) What did Lucy once use to bullet proof her chest?
   a. skillet
   b. garbage can lid
   c. cookie sheet
   d. oven door.

41) Why was the Ricardo apartment so cold the day ucy purchased a truckload of meat?

42) Lucy felt rejected when Ricky began buying gifts r the unborn baby. True or false?

43) What item did the Ricardos "sell" to the Mertzes?
   a. washing machine
   b. refrigerator
   c. vacuum cleaner
   d. television set

44) Ricky once told Lucy that "the charcoal would be ood for the baby's teeth." To what did this refer?

45) Ricky and Fred tried to discourage the girls from aking up golf by inventing their own set of rules. True r false?

46) Whose idea was it to retain a business manager—ucy's or Ricky's?

47) Complete the line that began, "Happy birthday, Irs. Mertz. I hope you live . . ."

48) Who was "the star upstairs" in Hollywood?

. . . Answers

740. a. skillet

741. Fred was fixing the furnace

742. True

743. a. washing machine

744. Waffles Ricky tried cooking for Lucy

745. True

746. Ricky's

747. "another seventy-five years"

748. Cornel Wilde

749) How did Lucy manage to obtain an authentic Richard Widmark souvenir?

750) Who called Lucy "a frowsy redhead"?

751) On the way to New York from Hollywood, the Ricardos stopped off to see cousin Ernie. True or false?

752) What singing group was featured on an episode warbling "Forever Darling"?

a. The Pied Pipers
b. The Modernaires
c. The Ames Brothers
d. The King Sisters

753) How did Lucy develop the cramp in her leg prior to meeting the Queen?

754) Who said, "Is it supposed to do that?"

755) Name Little Ricky's dog.

756) Who threatened to close down Lucy's raffle because she was not a charitable organization?

757) On the flight home from Europe, with whom did Ethel sit?

758) Approximately how many jars of salad dressing were sold?

a. 500
b. 1,000
c. 2,000
d. 3,000

. . . Answers

749. She scaled the wall surrounding his home

750. a newspaper reporter in Los Angeles

751. False, they visited him on the way to Los Angeles from New York

752. a. The Pied Pipers

753. She practiced her curtsy once too often

754. Ethel when she and Lucy were trying to change a flat tire

755. Fred

756. A representative of the New York City district attorney's office, Mr. Jamison

757. Fred

758. b. 1,000

759) Whom did Fred and Ethel impersonate at the end of the Richard Widmark episode?

760) To whom did Lucy once say, "You picked a fine one to tell you in plain English"?

761) After complaining that "you can't get a job in this town unless you can do something," Lucy got what job?

762) At what hotel were the Ricardos married a second time?

763) This actor played Ethel's dad. Name him.

764) Who advised Ricky "to climb in a hole and pull the hole in after him"?

765) What piece of fruit did Ricky sloppily eat after declaring that "a man's home is his castle"?

a. orange
b. apple
c. banana
d. pineapple

766) What was diner owner Watson's first name?

767) Who was Harvey Cromwell's assistant at the advertising agency?

768) What behind-the-scenes responsibility did Dann Cahn have on the show?

a. music composing
b. make-up
c. cinematography
d. filming editing

. . . Answers

759. Staff members of a mental institution

760. The foreman at the laundry

761. Babysitting the twins

762. The Eagle Hotel

763. Irving Bacon

764. Lucy after reading Ricky's horoscope in the newspaper

765. c. banana

766. Bill

767. Mr. Taylor

768. d. film editing

769) Who told Lucy she had to pay extra for her baby-wrapped cheese?

770) For his Connecticut calypso number, what type of drum did Little Ricky play?

771) When Jess Oppenheimer left the series in 1956, who, according to the show's credits, took over his responsibility?

772) Who was Mario's brother?
 a. Guido
 b. Salvatore
 c. Dominic
 d. Giuseppe

773) For her novel, Lucy renamed Ricky Nicky Ricardo. True or false?

774) When did Lucy proclaim that "there's a rotten Cuban in Denmark"?

775) What clause in the lease precipitated most of the trouble when the Ricardos decided to sublet their apartment?

776) With what episode would you associate Ethel's hostess pants?

777) Who caused all the confusion in Hollywood when Lucy thought Ricky stayed out all night?

. . . Answers

769. Airline stewardess

770. Bongos

771. Desi Arnaz, as producer

772. c. Dominic

773. False, Nicky Nicardo

774. When she discovered the trick Ricky played on her during the golf game

775. That the landlord must approve the sublessee

776. "Ethel's Birthday"

777. The hotel maid

778) What picture did Richard Widmark plug when he appeared on the show?

a. *A Prize of Gold*
b. *The Cobweb*
c. *Garden of Evil*
d. *Backlash*

779) Fred bought his motorcycle for fifty dollars. True or false?

780) When Lucy lost her acting assignment in an Italian film, who was tapped for the role?

781) Why did Mr. Hickox congratulate Lucy after reviewing her account books?

782) Who was Count Lorenzo?

783) Why did Lucy once consider herself "just a bit of flotsam in the sea"?

784) How much rice did Ricky cook when he and Fred agreed to take over the household chores?

785) How did Ricky make Lucy think she was turning green as a result of her so-called illness?

786) Whom did Lucy tell that "Dick and Oscar are just wild about" Ricky?

a. Mr. Cromwell
b. Mr. Reilly
c. Mr. Bennett
d. Mr. Meriweather

. . . Answers

778. a. *A Prize of Gold*

779. True

780. Ethel

781. Hers were the first set of books that had baffled him in twenty years

782. A character in Ricky's screen test script

783. When no one remembered her birthday

784. Four pounds

785. He installed a green light bulb

786. b. Mr. Reilly

787) When Ricky sold the Pontiac, he got more money than he paid for it. True or false?

788) Name Lucy's horse for the fox hunt.

789) Which hotel did the Ricardos stay at in London?
   a. Hotel Royale
   b. London Arms
   c. Plaza Hotel
   d. Hotel Berkshire

790) How did Lucy intend to "get the goods" on the Texas oilman and his spouse?

791) Name two "Lucy" characters who shared the surname "DuBois."

792) Why was Lucy's "Handy Dandy" vacuum cleaner originally so inexpensive?

793) How did Fred pay for the appliance he purchased from the Ricardos?
   a. cash
   b. check
   c. an I.O.U.
   d. none of the above

794) According to Ricky, what word is the same in English, Spanish, and French?

795) What was the more common title of "El Breako the Leaso"?

. . . Answers

787. True

788. Danny Boy

789. a. Hotel Royale

790. By surreptitiously tape-recording his claim that "oil stocks are as safe as U.S. government bonds"

791. Robert DuBois, a French waiter, and Charles Boyer's alias

792. Because she bought only the motor, nothing else

793. b. check

794. "No"

795. "La Raspa"

96) How did Ethel know that the first stranger at Lu-y's apartment was not sent by the radio show staff?

97) What new purchase did Lucy want to show Ethel n "Men Are Messy"?

a. a hat
b. bubble bath
c. perfume
d. a dress

98) What child's game did Lucy agree to play with the wins?

99) Who referred to Mr. Ritter as "the bee's knees"?

00) What was Professor Falconi's special talent?

01) Fred's mother was living. True or false?

02) Name the episode in which spirit gum played an mportant part.

03) How many separate times did Lucy knead the read dough?

04) Who was "King of the Konga"?

05) What was Ricky's secret for perfect creases in Lu-y's silk stockings?

06) Who taught Lucy how to act like a bop musician?

07) Which couple was not invited to Ricky and Fred's arewell party/Lucy and Ethel's baby shower?

a. Van Vlacks
b. Sedgwicks
c. Orsattis
d. Buzzells

. . . Answers

796. She caught the hobo rummaging through the trash barrel on the back porch

797. b. bubble bath

798. Here We Go 'Round the Maypole

799. Miss Lewis

800. Knife-throwing

801. True

802. "The Moustache"

803. Three

804. Xavier Valdez

805. He soaked them in starch

806. Fred

807. a. Van Vlacks

808) Grace Foster was a blonde. True or false?

809) Why did Sylvia Collins have to break her date with Eddie Collins?

810) According to Ethel, where did Fred get her wedding ring?

811) This actress played Marion Strong. Name her.

812) What episode featured a "challenge dance"?

813) What prompted Ethel to assume that Lucy was Madame X?

814) What did Lucy trade in her mink stole for?
- a. new furniture
- b. a vacation
- c. a home in the country
- d. none of the above

815) Who played Fred's old vaudeville partner?

816) What did the Hollywood hotel maid take one morning from the suite's bedroom wastepaper basket?

817) In "The Great Train Robbery," what role did actor Frank Nelson play?

818) At what point in Ricky's career did he acquire a formal talent agent?

819) What was the baggage limit on the transatlantic airplane flight?

. . . Answers

808. False, a brunette

809. She chipped a tooth

810. From a box of Cracker Jack

811. Shirley Mitchell

812. "Ricky's *Life* Story"

813. Mrs. Trumbull saw Lucy "steal" one of Fred's suits

814. a. new furniture

815. Charles Winninger

816. A carnation

817. Train conductor

818. After returning from Hollywood

819. Sixty-six pounds

820) Lucy purchased a hunk of rare Swiss cheese for her mother. True or false?

821) Name the American TV series that Charles Boyer was involved with.

822) At what Parisian cafe was Lucy arrested?

823) What song did the foursome play on bells at the rodeo show?

a. "Birmingham Jail"
b. "Home, Home on the Range"
c. "Down by the Old Mill Stream"
d. "She'll Be Comin' 'Round the Mountain"

824) Where did Lucy meet Rock Hudson?

825) Who was the 100th movie star that Lucy encountered in Hollywood?

826) When Ricky developed morning sickness, what doctor treated him?

827) Why did Lucy take up sculpting?

828) Where was the rodeo held?

829) Aside from Xavier, what name did Mrs. McGillicuddy call Ricky?

830) Edward R. Murrow played himself in "The Ricardos Are Interviewed." True or false?

831) Who once referred to Ethel as "medium raya"?

. . . Answers

820. False, Italian cheese

821. FOUR STAR PLAYHOUSE

822. A La Porte Montmartre

823. c. "Down by the Old Mill Stream"

824. In Palm Springs

825. Cornel Wilde

826. Dr. Rabwin

827. So her child would have an artistic influence

828. Madison Square Garden

829. Mickey

830. False

831. Fred in "The Seance"

832) What breed of dog did Richard Widmark own?

833) What did the drunk do to the diner owner at the end of "The Diner" episode?

834) Describe the design of Ethel's elaborate dress in "Charm School".

835) What song did Ricky's band play at the U.S. Customs Office upon their return from Europe?

836) What did Lucy pay for the "one-of-a-kind" oil painting she bought in Paris?

837) Who paid for the printing of the TV-set raffle tickets?

838) Barbara Pepper played the fat woman who sits on Lucy in the Hollywood tour bus. True or false?

839) What responsibility did Karl Freund have on the show?

840) What souvenir from Don the Beachcomber in Hollywood did Lucy manage to save?

a. chopsticks
b. napkin
c. menu
d. swizzle stick

841) What unusual item did Lucy and Ethel find in the trunk of Mrs. Grundy's car?

842) The Mertzes were Little Ricky's godparents. True or false?

. . . Answers

832. St. Bernard

833. Hit him with a custard pie

834. Leopard-skin off-the-shoulder dress

835. "Home Sweet Home"

836. 1000 francs

837. Mr. Feldman, the appliance store owner

838. False, Audrey Betz played the part

839. He was cinematographer

840. a. chopsticks

841. A hatchet

842. True

843) Whom did Ricky appoint as manager of the Tropicana when he bought it in 1956?

844) Lucy worked in a cigar store. True or false?

845) What disaster befell Lucy when she studied ballet?

846) What was Ricky's "fake illness"?

847) How much did it cost to move the giant freezer to the Mertz apartment building?

a. $25
b. $50
c. $100
d. $250

848) What tipped Ricky to the fact that the hillbilly in "The Girls Want to Go to a Nightclub" was really Lucy?

849) Ricky Ricardo, like his real life counterpart Desi Arnaz, appeared in Broadway's *Too Many Girls*. True or false?

850) What is *arroz con pollo*?

851) Where did Bill Foster live?

852) Who were Johnson, Miller, and Davis?

a. members of Ricky's band
b. the bald men Lucy hired
c. members of the Wednesday Afternoon Fine Arts League
d. none of the above

. . . Answers

843. Paul

844. True

845. Her foot got stuck in the practice bar

846. Amnesia

847. b. $50

848. She knew exactly where to find a pack of cigarettes

849. True

850. Chicken and rice

851. Apt. #2-A

852. b. the bald men Lucy hired

853) What "sliced, riced and diced"?

854) Who fired Mrs. Porter?

855) Who referred to Little Ricky as "a squawling brat"?

a. Mrs. Trumbull
b. Fred
c. Ethel
d. none of the above

856) When they realized they had purchased identical dresses, Lucy and Ethel both decide to return them. True or false?

857) What did Lucy contend was "only a passing fad, like goldfish-swallowing and flagpole-sitting"?

858) What was Lucy's response when the dance teacher suggested, "Let's go to the bar"?

859) At one time, Ricky was the manager of the Tropicana. True or false?

860) Who performed the song "Nobody Loves the Ump" with Lucy and Ricky?

861) Who were Larry Gleason, Diane Van Fossen, and Buddy Noble?

862) To what was Lucy referring when she said to Ethel, "After what I did last night, Cuba might cut off America's sugar supply"?

863) Ricky and the band played in Hawaii. True or false?

. . . Answers

853. A Handy Dandy Kitchen Helper

854. Ricky

855. c. Ethel

856. True

857. Television

858. "Good, I'm awfully thirsty"

859. True

860. Bob Hope

861. Members of Little Ricky's music school ensemble

862. Her disastrous first meeting with Uncle Alberto in Cuba

863. True

864) When did Ethel comment about Fred, "That's the most hair he's had in twenty years"?

865) What did Lucy wear on her head to impersonate Superman?

866) What did Lucy do when the helicopter pilot instructed her to "get ready" to board the *Constitution*?

867) What brand of cigarettes did the Ricardos smoke?

868) Under what circumstances was Lucy once referred to as a beekeeper?

869) According to Ethel, what word couldn't you "keep on your tongue even if you tried"?

870) The morning after Ricky's night out with the Hollywood starlets, where were the Mertzes and Lucy planning to go?

a. Farmer's Market
b. Knott's Berry Farm
c. Grauman's Chinese Theatre
d. Catalina Island

871) What was Fred's excuse for writing the phony "message from Hollywood," informing Ricky that he "got the job"?

872) According to Ricky, what did the initials C.B.S. stand for?

873) What language did Ethel intend to master before leaving for Europe?

. . . Answers

864. When Lucy accidentally painted his pate in "Redecorating the Mertzes' Apartment"

865. A football helmet

866. She repaired her makeup

867. Philip Morris

868. Wearing the loving cup and veil on her head in the subway

869. Lucy's proposed name for the dress shop, "Lucyeth's"

870. b. Knott's Berry Farm

871. He was "crazy with hunger"

872. Cuban Broadcasting System

873. Italian

874) What language did Fred intend to master before leaving for Europe?

875) What language did Lucy intend to master before leaving for Europe?

876) What did Ethel buy with the money she intended to spend on Fred's birthday present?

877) What gave Lucy away when she was trying to pose as a stone statue of a Minuteman?

878) Lucy got a little tipsy on wine in Paris. True or false?

879) What did Lucy once wash Ricky's suit in?

a. gasoline
b. water
c. kerosene
d. tomato juice

880) Name one song Ricky sang while Lucy was transferring the meat from the freezer to the furnace.

881) What song did Ricky sing while handcuffed to Lucy?

882) The Italian restaurant in "Equal Rights" was located on 39th Street near Tenth Avenue. True or false?

883) Who rented the Benson's apartment (#4-B) when they moved out of the building?

884) How many trips to Staten Island did Lucy and Fred take?

. . . Answers

874. German

875. French

876. New locks for the apartment house

877. The dog licked her face

878. False

879. b. water

880. “Cielito Lindo” or “Mama Inez”

881. “In Santiago, Chile”

882. False, near Eighth Avenue

883. Nancy and Sam Johnson

884. Five

385) In the final scene of "The Great Train Robbery," what were Fred and Ethel wearing?

386) Ricky's Hollywood film was never released. True or false?

387) Why did the U.S. Passport Office stay open to accommodate Lucy?

388) What did Lucy refer to as "a human pressure cooker"?

389) Who ran against Lucy as president of the women's club?

390) Who gave Ricky the silver cigarette case?

391) Where was the Hotel National?

a. London
b. Havana
c. Miami
d. Monte Carlo

392) The year "I Love Lucy" premiered, Lucille Ball appeared in the film *The Magic Carpet*. True or false?

393) Who played the interviewer from the fan magazine?

394) Who was the nephew of the woman who ran the French hand laundry?

395) How did Fred make money from Ricky's celebrity?

. . . Answers

885. Plastic raincoats

886. False; it opened at Radio City Music Hall

887. Because Fred unplugged the clock

888. The steam cabinet in "The Diet"

889. Ethel

890. The boys in the band

891. b. Havana

892. True

893. Joan Banks

894. Jean Valjean Raymand

895. He started selling Ricky's personal items like old BVDs, etc.

896) How did Superman burst into the room to surprise birthday boy Ricky and his young friends?

897) What was the Mertzes' gift to Lucy and Ricky for their thirteenth wedding anniversary?

898) What did William Holden have for lunch the day he met Lucy Ricardo?

899) What was producer Parker's first name?
a. Sam
b. Bill
c. Jerry
d. Paul

900) Where did Lucy and the Mertzes read the item announcing the cancellation of Ricky's film?

901) Caroline Appleby had a severe case of nearsightedness. True or false?

902) What was Lucy doing hiding under a room service cart at her Hollywood hotel?

903) Who continually prevented Lucy from "drowning" in the Hollywood hotel pool?

904) Lucy once read in the newspaper that a housewife "made a fortune" doing this. What?

905) What song did Ricky sing in his "Ricky Ricardo Presents Tropical Rhythms" pilot?
a. "Vaya con Dios"
b. "Guadalajara"
c. "Babalu"
d. "El Cumbanchero"

. . . Answers

896. He entered via the louvre windows that separated the Ricardo living room from the kitchen

897. A cigarette lighter, and, technically, a party

898. A Cobb Salad

899. b. Bill

900. *Variety*

901. True

902. Trying to gain admittance to Cornel Wilde's suite

903. The hotel lifeguard

904. Writing a book

905. a. "Vaya con Dios"

906) Name the musical Parker was producing.

907) When Ricky decided to go camping, Lucy started reading what section of the newspaper?

908) Why did the scenery rental film confiscate the sets used in the operetta?

909) Fred never wore a toupee. True or false?

910) What political office did actress Elizabeth Patterson once play on I LOVE LUCY?

911) Name the orchestra member whom Ricky called a "wolf."

912) What fictional TV show did Millikan's sponsor?

913) Can you name any one of the MGM remake movies Lucy suggested as vehicles for Ricky?

914) Lucy told an interviewer that she graduated high school in 1940. True or false?

915) What did Ricky forbid Lucy to do the day he was waiting for the call from Hollywood?

916) Describe Lucy's physical appearance when she returned to the hotel after confiscating John Wayne's concrete slab.

917) Aside from tearful goodbyes, what else did the Ricardos and Mertzes exchange when Lucy and Ricky moved to the country?

. . . Answers

906. *The Professor and the Coed*

907. Sports

908. Lucy's post-dated check bounced

909. False, he wore one briefly in "Lucy Thinks Ricky's Getting Bald"

910. Mayor of a small town in Connecticut

911. Joe Gutierrez, the trombone player

912. "Chicken Mash Hour"

913. *Gone with the Cuban Wind, It Happened One Noche, Andy Hardy Meets a Conga Player, Meet Me in St. Ricky*, and *Ricky's Son of Flicka*

914. False, she told her she graduated four years after she started

915. Use the telephone

916. Her foot was stuck in a pail of hardened cement

917. House keys

918) Who gave Little Ricky a puppy?
- a. Fred and Ethel
- b. The Applebys
- c. Mrs. Trumbull
- d. Billy Palmer

919) Who played the Yankee Stadium hotdog vendor?

920) Who was Nancy Graham?

921) What day of the week did the Wednesday Afternoon Fine Arts League meet?
- a. Wednesday
- b. Thursday
- c. Friday
- d. Saturday

922) What song did Lucy and Van Johnson perform?

923) Ethel Mertz was never sued in court. True or false?

924) What type of phone service did the Ricardos have?

925) Under what circumstances did Ricky tell Lucy, "You're sure going out true to form"?

926) Whose friend was Eddie Grant?
- a. Lucy's
- b. Ricky's
- c. Fred's
- d. Ethel's

927) What did Ricky once put on a slice of bread that caused Lucy to observe, "I'll never get used to your strange Cuban ways"?

. . . Answers

918. d. Billy Palmer

919. Lucy and/or Bennett Green

920. Newspaper reporter in "Homecoming"

921. c. Friday

922. "How About You?"

923. False; she and Fred were sued by the Ricardos in "The Courtroom"

924. Party line

925. When they were stranded in the cabin in the Alps

926. c. Fred's

927. Butter

928) Who were "the world's greatest contortionists"?

929) What did Lucy serve Mr. Ritter as a beverage at dinner?

930) The little boy twins wore matching hats. True or false?

931) What did Lucy want to eat while waiting to go to the hospital?

a. sandwich
b. tea and toast
c. hot chocolate
d. milk and cookies

932) What was the recommended dosage of Vitameatavegamin?

933) Who played the role of Hedda Hopper?

934) Who was the Vitameatavegamin commercial script-clerk?

935) What equipment did Lucy and Ethel take to Grauman's Chinese Theatre?

936) When Ethel read Lucy's fortune with a deck of playing cards, what particular card represented Lucy?

937) Ethel once asked for a divorce. True or false?

938) What happened to the record of "Mamo Yo Quiero" when Lucy was lip-syncing the lyrics?

939) How did Lucy and the other dance hopefuls audition for the "Sally Sweet" number?

. . . Answers

928. Pugh and Carroll

929. Tomato juice . . . still in the can

930. True

931. d. milk and cookies

932. "A tablespoon after every meal"

933. Hedda Hopper played herself

934. Maury

935. A crowbar and a bucket of cement

936. Queen of hearts

937. False, Lucy asked in her behalf but Ethel said no

938. The phonograph played it at uneven speeds

939. They had to do the time-step

940) Who urged Lucy to attend the radio show, "Females Are Fabulous"?

941) What famous real-life TV couple did Lucy use as an example when she tried to convince Ricky to use her for his TV show audition?

942) During the seance, what device did Ethel employ?

943) What stuffed animal did Lucy wield in "Men Are Messy"?

944) From what era in American history was Fred's military uniform in "Drafted"?

a. Civil War
b. American Revolution
c. World War I
d. World War II

945) A burglar once stole a fur coat from Lucy. True or false?

946) On what occasion did Lucy and Ricky sing "We'll Build a Bungalow"?

947) During the Ricardos and Mertzes' frequent songfests, who usually played the piano?

948) What classic burlesque routine was Lucy taught by a veteran clown?

949) What was Lucy's scheme to discourage the Ricardos' "fans," Peggy and Arthur?

. . . Answers

940. Ethel

941. George Burns and Gracie Allen

942. A crystal ball

943. A bear

944. a. Civil War

945. False

946. At Ethel's women's club benefit

947. Ricky or Ethel

948. Slowly I Turn

949. To make her and Ricky look much older than they were

950) How did the Ricardos and Mertzes spy on the new thespian couple when they were moving into the apartment building?

951) What did Lucy once ultimately do when she thought her apartment was on fire?

952) Lucy once pasted a moustache on her face to teach Ricky a lesson. True or false?

953) What did Ricky and Fred bet the girls that they couldn't live like their pioneer ancestors?

a. new hats
b. $50
c. $100
d. a vacation

954) Where did Lucy stash the loot she was collecting for her women's club bazaar?

955) Why was Lucy *not* jealous when she first heard Ricky talk about Renita Perez?

956) What was Lucy's response to the quiz show question, "What is a senator's term of office?"

957) How many other job offers did Lucy claim Ricky had when she urged him to ask for a raise?

a. two
b. six
c. ten
d. twelve

958) In what position did Lucy and Ricky sleep when they were handcuffed to each other?

. . . Answers

950. Using a pair of binoculars, they watched them and their moving van from the Ricardo living room window

951. She jumped out of the bedroom window

952. False, she pasted a beard on her face

953. b. $50

954. In the living room closet

955. The last time Ricky saw Renita she was still a little girl but that was at least a dozen years ago

956. "The sap runs every two years"

957. d. twelve

958. Prone position with their heads at the foot of the bed

959) Where did Lucy and Ethel live when they took their "vacation from marriage"?

960) Lucy produced a flapper-themed show at the Tropicana. True or false?

961) Why did Ricky fire the psychiatrist he hired to help Lucy alleviate her inferiority complex?

962) How did Lucy describe the office of the women's club vice-president?

963) Ricky sent Lucy flowers to apologize for giving her a black eye. True or false?

964) Name Tom Henderson's brother.
a. Herman
b. Harry
c. Harvey
d. Henry

965) What scheme did Lucy and Ethel dream up to get rid of the bossy maid?

966) What did Lucy and Ethel do when two actors dressed as Indians showed up at the Ricardo apartment one day?

967) Where did Ethel say she was going the night of Lucy's birthday?

. . . Answers

959. At the Mertzes' apartment

960. True

961. The doctor made a pass at Lucy

962. "Merely a figurehead"

963. False, Fred sent them for Ricky but mistakenly signed his own name to the accompanying card

964. b. Harry

965. They turned the Ricardo apartment into a "pig pen" so the servant would get so disgusted, she'd quit

966. They hit them over the head, knocking them out

967. To dinner with Fred and his lodge president

968) What was the first item Lucy carried downstairs when she switched apartments?

a. coffee table
b. desk blotter
c. lamp
d. pen

969) When Ricky admonished Lucy about her "stravaganzas," what did she do the next morning at breakfast to retaliate?

970) How did Lucy use up all the water in the canteen when she and Ricky went camping?

971) Why did Lucy once believe that Little Ricky would forget her name when he got older?

972) In "Never Do Business with Friends," who finally paid for the washing machine?

973) Lucy and Ethel once opened a hat shop. True or false?

974) How did Lucy create the sound of a gunshot in "Equal Rights"?

975) What did Lucy call Stevie Appleby's playpen?

976) What question did "truthful" Lucy's friends *not* ask her?

a. her age
b. her weight
c. her true hair color
d. her dress size

. . . Answers

968. b. desk blotter

969. She served him a breakfast made up of a teeny egg and a speck of sausage

970. She washed her hair with it

971. Because she was not as "famous" as Ricky, worsened by the fact that her face was missing from a *Life* magazine story

972. The Ricardos and Mertzes split the cost

973. False; a dress shop

974. By blowing up a paper bag and popping it

975. His "cage"

976. d. her dress size

977) Who once said to Fred, "If the penny fits, pinch it"?

978) Fred once was mistaken for a bum. True or false?

979) Who instigated the meeting between Carlota and Ricky?

980) Why did Ricky start crying when Lucy began making salad dressing?

981) When asked by the charm school operator to provide a voice check, what did Lucy respond?

982) How many people were on the Tropicana mailing list?

a. 3,000
b. 4,000
c. 5,000
d. 6,000

983) Lucy sometimes used her maiden name. True or false?

984) What did the Mertzes do when Ricky showed his home movies?

985) Who sponsored the bonus buck contest?

986) Lucy was afraid to sit in the dentist's chair. True or false?

. . . Answers

977. Ethel

978. True

979. Jerry, Ricky's press agent

980. She was cutting up onions and he was sitting nearby

981. "Testing, one, . . . two, . . . three, . . . testing"

982. a. 3,000

983. True

984. They snuck out of the apartment

985. A newspaper

986. False, the eye doctor's chair

987) Where did Lucy and Ethel learn of the martian jobs?

a. *The New York Times*
b. *Variety*
c. *Billboard*
d. Cynthia Harcourt

988) Who was Mr. Dorrance?

989) Where did the Wednesday Afternoon Fine Arts League band rehearse?

990) Why did the Ricardos and the Mertzes divide the diner in half?

991) Sporting a black wig, where did "date" Lucy meet Ricky for dinner?

992) What "sure fire" scheme did the Ricardos first hatch to get Ernie to go back to Bent Fork?

993) The oil well the Ricardos and Mertzes originally invested in was a gusher. True or false?

994) What prompted Lucy's paranoia over Ricky's devotion in "Lucy Cries Wolf"?

995) What role did actress Sarah Selby play?

996) After being put on a strict budget by a business manager, how did Ricky manage to pay for his haircut and shave?

. . . Answers

987. c. *Billboard*

988. A book publisher

989. At Ethel's

990. Because Fred and Ethel were fed up doing all the hard work

991. At Tony's, an Italian restaurant

992. They bought a bus ticket back to Bent Fork and purposely "lost" it in the apartment house hallway, hoping Ernie would find it . . . and use it

993. True

994. She read a newspaper account of a woman whose husband ignored her in her time of dire need

995. Dorothy Cooke

996. Lucy gave him the necessary cash

997) Why did Lucy sabotage the husband-and-wife television show?

998) How was the old Mertz and Kurtz act billed?

999) Where did the Hollywood talent scout reside while in New York City casting *Don Juan*?

a. at a hotel
b. at the Ricardos'
c. at the Applebys'
d. at the M-G-M suite at the Waldorf

1000) Who played the director of Ricky's screen test?

1001) Who played Little Ricky's *abuela*?

1002) After Ricky's screen test, how long did it take M-G-M to make the decision to cast him for the *Don Juan* lead?

1003) Before leaving for Hollywood, Lucy arranged for car insurance for the Pontiac. True or false?

1004) What time of the morning did Ricky hope to depart on the auto trip to California?

1005) At the rundown motel in the midwest, who eventually slept on the bunk beds?

1006) When Ethel's father informed her that her old bedroom hadn't been touched since she left, what was Fred's retort?

. . . Answers

997. To get even with Ricky, who didn't really want her involved with it at all

998. "Laugh 'til It Hurts with Mertz and Kurtz"

999. a. at a hotel

1000. Clinton Sundberg

1001. Mary Emery

1002. Two weeks

1003. False, Ricky did the chore

1004. six o'clock

1005. Lucy and Ricky

1006. "It must be a dusty mess by now"

1007) Who had use of the car their first day in Hollywood—Lucy or Ricky?

1008) Who were Beverly, Dolores, Shirlee, and Maggie?

1009) How did Lucy finally get her name on the silver screen?

1010) Ricky attended Lucy's Hollywood fashion show. True or false?

1011) How many fan letters did Lucy, the Mertzes and Mrs. McGillicuddy write in order to convince M-G-M to renew Ricky's option?

a. 100
b. 250
c. 500
d. 1,000

1012) Name the foursome's bell-chiming act at the rodeo.

1013) What "charitable" organization did Lucy and Ethel invent to raise money for their trip to Europe?

1014) Lucy and Fred fell asleep on the ferry because they took too many seasickness pills. True or false?

1015) How was Lucy freed from the ship's porthole in which she got herself stuck?

1016) Whose autograph did Lucy get in the lobby of her London hotel?

. . . Answers

1007. Lucy

1008. The Hollywood starlets Ricky escorted to a movie premiere

1009. She wrote LUCY RICARDO on the soles of her shoes

1010. False, Ethel attended

1011. c. 500

1012. Lucille Cannonball McGillicuddy and Her Western Bell-Ringers

1013. Ladies Overseas Aid

1014. True

1015. Acetylene torches

1016. Ricky's

1017) Lucy picked up her mother and Little Ricky at the airport upon the pair's arrival in Los Angeles. True or false?

1018) How did Ethel tell Charles Boyer to get the ink stains off his shirt?

1019) Trapped in the Swiss Alps, who was the last to hear the sound of the approaching Bavarian band?

a. Lucy
b. Ricky
c. Fred
d. Ethel

1020) Where in Italy was Lucy when Little Ricky celebrated his birthday back in the states?

1021) Name the Italian filmmaker whom Lucy encountered in Italy.

1022) What number did Lucy plaster on herself for the so-called bicycle race in Europe?

1023) What game did Lucy "play" in Monte Carlo?

1024) Whose relative was Uncle Elmo?

1025) What was Lucy's response to the question, "Did you stop this train by pulling that handle?"

. . . Answers

1017. False, Hedda Hopper gave her a lift to Lucy's hotel

1018. By using milk

1019. c. Fred

1020. Florence

1021. Vittorio Felipe

1022. 25

1023. Roulette

1024. Ethel's

1025. "I didn't do it by draggin' my foot!"

MORE BESTSELLING ROMANCE BY JANELLE TAYLOR

SAVAGE CONQUEST (1533, $3.75)
Having heeded her passionate nature and stolen away to the rugged plains of South Dakota, the Virginia belle Miranda was captured there by a handsome, virile Indian. As her defenses melted with his burning kisses she didn't know what to fear more: her fate at the hands of the masterful brave, or her own traitorous heart!

FIRST LOVE, WILD LOVE (1431, $3.75)
Roused from slumber by the most wonderful sensations, Calinda's pleasure turned to horror when she discovered she was in a stranger's embrace. Handsome cattle baron Lynx Cardone had assumed she was in his room for his enjoyment, and before Calinda could help herself his sensuous kisses held her under the spell of desire!

GOLDEN TORMENT (1323, $3.75)
The instant Kathryn saw Landis Jurrell she didn't know what to fear more: the fierce, aggressive lumberjack or the torrid emotions he ignited in her. She had travelled to the Alaskan wilderness to search for her father, but after one night of sensual pleasure Landis vowed never to let her travel alone!

LOVE ME WITH FURY (1248, $3.75)
The moment Captain Steele saw golden-haired Alexandria swimming in the hidden pool he vowed to have her—but she was outraged he had intruded on her privacy. But against her will his tingling caresses and intoxicating kisses compelled her to give herself to the ruthless pirate, helplessly murmuring, "LOVE ME WITH FURY!"

TENDER ECSTASY (1212, $3.75)
Bright Arrow is committed to kill every white he sees—until he sets his eyes on ravishing Rebecca. And fate demands that he capture her, torment her . . . and soar with her to the dizzying heights of TENDER ECSTASY!

Available wherever paperbacks are sold, or order direct from the Publisher. Send cover price plus 50¢ per copy for mailing and handling to Zebra Books, Dept. 1730, 475 Park Avenue South, New York, N.Y. 10016. DO NOT SEND CASH.